Better Homes and Gardens®

So-Good Meals Cook Book

© Meredith Corporation, 1975. All Rights Reserved.
Printed in the United States of America. First Edition. First Printing.
Library of Congress Catalog Card Number: 74-25581
SBN: 696-00830-0

Contents

This section offers a host of quick-to-fix and make-ahead recipe specialties for people who have little time for meal preparation. The menus are all planned for keeping a hectic schedule under control. Included are speedy skillet dinners, short-cut soups and chowders, tasty sandwiches, and fast desserts.

If you are the type who enjoys picnics, backyard cook-outs, or on-location camp cooking, you'll like this section. Barbecued kabobs and burgers, summertime salads, grill-size vegetables, bread fix-ups, and thirst-quenching beverages are all excellent choices for the hungry outdoor enthusiast.

Let the whole family take credit for a delicious meal. This section features recipes and menus that all of the family members—even Dad—can help you prepare. Make selections from enticing pizzas and sandwiches, impressive salads and vegetables, and homemade ice cream.

Meals That Save Dollars

The money-saving recipes in this section are geared for the thrifty-minded. Tasty crockery-cooking recipes and some interesting ideas for using leftovers are also included. Delight your family with delicious casseroles, bread puddings, and appealing main dishes created from leftover foods.

On the cover: As an accompaniment for the *Glazed Turkey Roast* (see recipe, page 56), serve scoops of cooked, mashed sweet potatoes garnished with snipped parsley. Top the turkey roast with slices of canned or poached, fresh purple plums.

BETTER HOMES AND GARDENS BOOKS

Editorial Director: Don Dooley
Managing Editor: Malcolm E. Robinson   Art Director: John Berg
Asst. Managing Editor: Lawrence D. Clayton   Asst. Art Director: Randall Yontz
Food Editor: Nancy Morton
Senior Food Editor: Joyce Trollope
Associate Editors: Sandra Granseth, Sharyl Heiken, Rosemary C. Hutchinson, Elizabeth Strait
Assistant Editors: Diane Jesse, Catherine Penney
Designers: Faith Berven, Candy Carleton, Harijs Priekulis

Our seal assures you that every recipe in *So-Good Meals Cook Book* is endorsed by the Better Homes and Gardens Test Kitchen. Each recipe is tested for family appeal, practicality, and deliciousness.

Introduction

The purpose of *Better Homes and Gardens So-Good Meals Cook Book* is to provide you with a multitude of tested recipes and interesting menu ideas that will help you create superb meals of excellent quality.

In every respect, this book is as versatile as you are. And with the many activities that make demands on your time, you need a cook book that can handle any cooking situation you find yourself in.

If you're one of the many people who are short on mealtime preparation, you will appreciate the first recipe section. In it, you'll find recipes that you can cook ahead and store in the refrigerator a day before you need them, plus many dishes you can prepare in a jiffy.

When you are pursuing the great outdoor life, choose some of the delicacies from the second section. These recipes and menus are ideal for backyard barbecues, picnic outings, patio suppers, backpack trips and just about any other activity you can mention.

Today, more and more families are finding that cooking together is great fun. So, if your family enjoys getting involved and helping prepare meals, be sure to pay special attention to the third section.

In the last section, the recipes are geared to assist you in keeping your food budget in line and to help you make the most of your time. Cost-cutting recipes, crockery cooking, and imaginative ways for putting leftovers to good use— they're all included here.

◀ **Island Sweet-Sour Meatballs** served over fluffy hot cooked rice makes a delightfully tempting main dish for your family. The juicy meatballs are a ground beef-textured vegetable protein mixture. (See recipe, page 76.)

Meals for People on the Go

Impress your family and weekend guests with a spectacular luncheon on your patio. Tempt appetites with Fruit and Turkey Platter, Hot Curried Rice Salad, and a basket of Fluffy Graham Muffins served warm with butter. (See index for recipe pages.)

Menus for Busy People

Steak and Vegetable Kabobs

1 cup Burgundy
¼ cup cooking oil
2 tablespoons onion soup mix
1 teaspoon salt
½ teaspoon dried thyme, crushed
¼ teaspoon pepper
1 small clove garlic, minced
2 pounds beef sirloin steak,
   cut in 1-inch pieces
• • •
2 zucchini, cut in 1-inch slices
2 ears corn, cut in 1-inch
   slices
Cherry tomatoes

In bowl combine Burgundy, oil, dry onion soup mix, salt, thyme, pepper, and garlic. Add meat pieces and stir to coat well. Cover and marinate at room temperature for 2 hours, or overnight in refrigerator. Drain meat, reserving marinade. Salt vegetables.

On 6 skewers thread the meat pieces alternately with slices of zucchini and corn. Broil the kabobs 4 to 6 inches from heat for 4 minutes. Make a quarter turn and brush with additional marinade; broil 4 minutes more. Repeat turning and brushing 2 more times till all sides are browned. Garnish end of each skewer with a cherry tomato. Makes 6 servings.

Parsley Rice

In a saucepan combine 2 cups cold water, 1 cup long grain rice, and ½ teaspoon salt; cover with tight-fitting lid. Bring to a rolling boil; reduce heat. Continue cooking 14 minutes (do not lift cover). Remove from heat; let stand, covered, 10 minutes. Stir in 2 tablespoons snipped parsley. Makes 3 cups.

Steak and Vegetable Kabobs, broiled to perfection and served on a bed of *Parsley Rice*, is a delicious, quick-to-fix main dish. Serve the *Parmesan-Topped Loaves* hot from the oven. ▶

KABOB DINNER

Steak and Vegetable Kabobs
Parsley Rice
Crisp Salad Greens French Dressing
Parmesan-Topped Loaves Butter
or
Breadsticks
Lime Sherbet
Coffee   Milk

Special Helps: To enhance the flavor of the steak pieces, marinate them in a wine and oil mixture seasoned with herbs for 2 hours before cooking—overnight is better. At serving time, arrange the kabobs on the platter of cooked rice.

Parmesan-Topped Loaves

1 loaf frozen white
   bread dough (1 pound)
Shortening
• • •
¼ cup grated Parmesan cheese
Cornmeal

Rub the frozen loaf with shortening. Thaw the dough for 1½ to 2 hours at room temperature. With knife, cut dough into six equal pieces. Shape each piece into miniature loaf about 3x1½ inches. Brush each loaf lightly with cold water. Roll the top of each loaf in some of the cheese. Place loaves on a greased baking sheet that has been sprinkled with cornmeal. Let dough rise till almost double (30 minutes).

Place a shallow pan on lower rack of oven; fill pan with boiling water. Sprinkle the top of each loaf with cold water. Then, sprinkle each with the remaining cheese. Bake at 350° till golden brown, 25 to 30 minutes. Serve warm. Makes 6 loaves.

JIFFY PORK DINNER

Vegetable-Pork Cups
Spiced Mandarin Mold
Hard Rolls   Butter
Choco-Mint Freeze
Coffee   Milk

Special Helps: Want to prepare cooked pork in a different, easy-to-fix way? Then, serve Vegetable-Pork Cups. It will take you just a few minutes to heat the pork-vegetable mixture, leaving plenty of time to prepare the stuffing shells and unmold the gelatin salad.

Vegetable-Pork Cups

    2 tablespoons butter *or*
        margarine
    3 cups herb-seasoned stuffing
        mix
    1 beaten egg
    ½ cup water
        • • •
    2 10-ounce packages frozen
        Chinese-style vegetables
    2 cups diced cooked pork
    1 cup cold water
    4 teaspoons cornstarch
    1 tablespoon soy sauce

In saucepan melt butter or margarine. Remove from heat; add the herb-seasoned stuffing mix. Combine beaten egg and the ½ cup water; add to butter-stuffing mixture in the saucepan. Toss mixture well to combine. Press stuffing mixture into bottom and up onto sides of six lightly greased 1-cup casseroles. Bake cups at 425° for 10 minutes.

Meanwhile, cook the Chinese-style vegetables according to package directions. Add pork. Blend the 1 cup water, cornstarch, and soy sauce; add to the vegetable-pork mixture. Cook and stir till mixture is thickened and bubbly. Spoon the hot vegetable-pork mixture into the baked stuffing cups. Makes 6 servings.

Spiced Mandarin Mold

    1 11-ounce can mandarin orange
        sections
    6 inches stick cinnamon
    ½ teaspoon whole cloves
    1 6-ounce package lemon-
        flavored gelatin
    1 cup orange juice
    ½ cup chopped pecans
        Lettuce

Advance preparation: Drain orange sections, reserving syrup. Add water to syrup to make 1¾ cups. In saucepan combine syrup mixture, cinnamon, cloves, and ¼ teaspoon salt. Cover and simmer 15 minutes. Add gelatin to syrup mixture; stir over low heat till gelatin is dissolved. Strain out stick cinnamon and cloves. Add orange juice and 1 cup cold water. Chill till partially set. Fold in drained oranges and pecans; turn into a 5-cup mold. Chill salad till firm, 4 hours or overnight. **Before serving:** Unmold the salad on a lettuce-lined plate. Makes 8 servings.

Choco-Mint Freeze

    1¼ cups finely crushed
        vanilla wafers
    ¼ cup butter *or* margarine,
        melted
    1 quart peppermint stick ice
        cream, softened
    ½ cup butter *or* margarine
    2 1-ounce squares unsweetened
        chocolate
    3 well-beaten egg yolks
    1½ cups sifted powdered sugar
    1 teaspoon vanilla
    3 egg whites

Advance preparation: Toss together crumbs and ¼ cup melted butter. Reserve ¼ cup crumb mixture; press remaining crumb mixture into 9x9x2-inch baking pan. Spread with ice cream; freeze. Meanwhile, melt ½ cup butter and chocolate over low heat; gradually stir into yolks with the sugar and vanilla. Cool well. Beat whites till stiff peaks form. Beat chocolate mixture till smooth; fold in egg whites. Spread chocolate mixture over ice cream. Top with reserved crumbs; freeze. Serves 8.

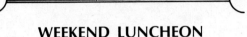

WEEKEND LUNCHEON

(See photo, page 6)

Fruit and Turkey Platter
Hot Curried Rice Salad
Fluffy Graham Muffins   Butter
Tea   Coffee

Special Helps: The weekends allow more time to prepare and serve a leisurely lunch. Take advantage of the extra time to make this a special meal.

First, prepare the fresh pineapple by cutting into spears and chilling. An elegant way to serve leftover turkey is with a fruit platter. Slice, wrap, and refrigerate the turkey. Then, stir up and bake the muffins. All that's left to do is prepare the remaining fruit and cook the rice salad; then serve your guests.

Hot Curried Rice Salad

    2 cups water
    2 teaspoons instant chicken
        bouillon granules
    1 teaspoon curry powder
    ½ teaspoon salt
    1 cup long grain rice
    ⅓ cup raisins
    1 3-ounce can sliced mushrooms,
        drained
    1 10-ounce package frozen peas
    2 tablespoons butter *or*
        margarine
    1 tablespoon chopped canned
        pimiento

In saucepan bring water, bouillon granules, curry powder, and salt to boiling. Stir in rice; cover and reduce heat to low. Cook 14 minutes. Add raisins and mushrooms; remove from heat and let stand, covered, for 10 minutes. Meanwhile, cook peas following package directions; drain. Add to rice mixture along with butter and pimiento; toss to mix. Turn into serving bowl. Makes 6 servings.

Fruit and Turkey Platter

    1 pineapple
    1 pint strawberries
    3 avocados
      Lemon juice
    6 tablespoons chutney
    3 bananas
    ½ cup coarsely chopped nuts

    • • •

      Lettuce
    6 slices cooked turkey, chilled

Rinse pineapple. Twist off the crown and cut off the base. Slice off strips of rind lengthwise, then remove eyes of fruit by cutting away. Cut off the hard core of pineapple as you slice the fruit in spears. Save some of the juice, if possible. Cover spears; chill. Just before serving, thoroughly rinse the whole strawberries with caps attached by swirling through cold water. Drain the berries well. Rinse the avocados. Cut each fruit lengthwise and twist gently to separate the halves and lift out the seed. Brush the cut surfaces with the reserved pineapple juice or lemon juice to keep the fruit from darkening. Chill thoroughly. Before serving, fill each half with *1 tablespoon* of the chutney.

Peel bananas and cut in 1½-inch chunks. Brush the chunks with the pineapple juice or lemon juice to prevent darkening. Roll the chunks lightly in the coarsely chopped nuts. Just before serving time arrange the fresh fruit on a lettuce-lined serving platter; add the turkey slices. Makes 6 servings.

Fluffy Graham Muffins

    1¼ cups all-purpose flour
     ½ cup whole wheat flour
     ¼ cup sugar
    2½ teaspoons baking powder
     ¾ teaspoon salt
      1 beaten egg
     ¾ cup buttermilk
     ⅓ cup cooking oil

Stir together flours, sugar, baking powder, and salt; make well in center. Mix egg, buttermilk, and oil; add to dry ingredients. Stir to moisten. Fill greased muffin pans ⅔ full. Bake at 400° for 20 to 25 minutes. Makes 12.

Recipes Within Your Schedule

Beef and Cheese Lasagne

6 lasagne noodles (3 ounces)
½ pound ground beef
½ cup chopped onion
1 clove garlic, minced
1 8-ounce can tomatoes, cut up
1 8-ounce can tomato sauce
1 3-ounce can sliced mushrooms,
    drained
¼ teaspoon dried basil,
    crushed
1 cup ricotta *or* cream-style
    cottage cheese
½ cup grated Gouda *or* Edam
    cheese (2 ounces)
2 teaspoons dried parsley flakes
4 ounces sliced Swiss cheese

Advance preparation: Cook noodles according to package directions; drain. Cook beef, onion, and garlic till beef is browned and onion is tender; drain off fat. Combine beef mixture, undrained tomatoes, tomato sauce, mushrooms, and basil. Bring to boiling. Mix ricotta, Gouda, and parsley. Place *half* the noodles in 10x6x2-inch baking dish, folding under to fit dish. Spread with *half* the cheese mixture; top with *half* the Swiss cheese. Cover with *half* the beef mixture; repeat. Cover; refrigerate up to 24 hours.
Before serving: Bake, covered, at 375° for 1 hour. Uncover and bake about 10 minutes longer. Let stand 10 minutes. Makes 6 servings.

Saucy Shrimp Skillet

In medium saucepan cook one 10-ounce package frozen Chinese-style vegetables according to package directions. Do not drain. Stir in one 10½-ounce can cream of shrimp soup, ¼ cup dry sherry, and one 3-ounce can sliced mushrooms, drained. Cook mixture till bubbly. Drain and rinse one 4½-ounce can shrimp. Carefully stir shrimp into sauce mixture. Heat through and serve over hot cooked rice. Sprinkle with toasted slivered almonds. Makes 4 servings.

Gazpacho-Meat Meal

1 5½-ounce can tomato juice
    (¾ cup)
½ slice bread, torn in pieces
1 tablespoon salad oil
1 tablespoon wine vinegar
¼ teaspoon salt
    Dash garlic salt
    Dash pepper
1 medium tomato, cut up
½ cup finely chopped celery
¼ cup finely chopped
    green pepper
2 tablespoons finely
    chopped onion
1 tablespoon finely snipped
    parsley
• • •
6 cups mixed salad greens
2 medium tomatoes,
    cut in wedges
1 medium cucumber,
    thinly sliced
1 cup sliced radishes
    Lettuce
12 ounces assorted cold cuts

Advance preparation: For salad dressing, in a blender container combine tomato juice, torn bread pieces, salad oil, wine vinegar, salt, garlic salt, pepper, and *half* of the 1 medium tomato. Cover the blender container and blend mixture well. Finely chop the remaining tomato; add to the blended tomato juice mixture. Stir in chopped celery, green pepper, onion, and the snipped parsley. *Do not blend.*

Transfer the salad dressing to a serving bowl. Cover; refrigerate till serving time.
Before serving: In large bowl combine mixed salad greens, the 2 medium tomatoes, cucumber, and sliced radishes. Turn the mixture into a lettuce-lined salad bowl.

Arrange cold cuts on serving platter with the bowl of salad dressing in the center. Roll up a few slices of meat and place on platter. Then, pour some of the dressing over the salad, tossing lightly. Makes 6 servings.

Gazpacho-Meat Meal can rescue you on a hot summer's day because it's all keep-cool cooking. Using garden-fresh vegetables, prepare the salad dressing ahead and chill. Just prior to mealtime, arrange a platter of cold cuts around the dressing and serve with salad.

Italian-Seasoned Pork Chops

6 pork loin chops, cut ¾ to
   1 inch thick
2 tablespoons cooking oil
1 envelope Italian salad
   dressing mix
½ cup dry red wine
½ cup water
2 tablespoons cold water
4 teaspoons cornstarch
   Hot cooked spaghetti *or*
   noodles

In large skillet slowly brown the chops in hot oil. Add Italian salad dressing mix, wine, and the ½ cup water. Cover and simmer till chops are tender, 30 to 40 minutes.

Remove the chops to serving platter; keep warm. Measure pan juices; add water if necessary to equal 1¼ cups. Blend the 2 tablespoons cold water slowly into cornstarch. Stir into pan juices. Cook and stir till thickened and bubbly. Serve the chops with gravy and hot cooked spaghetti or noodles. Serves 6.

Sausage-Noodle Skillet

1 pound bulk pork sausage
1½ cups water
1 16-ounce can tomatoes,
   cut up
1 15½-ounce can red kidney
   beans, drained
1 8-ounce can tomato sauce
½ cup chopped green pepper
2 teaspoons instant minced
   onion
1 to 2 teaspoons chili powder
½ teaspoon salt
4 ounces uncooked medium
   noodles (about 2½ cups)

In skillet cook the pork sausage till meat is browned. Drain off the excess fat. Stir in water, undrained tomatoes, red kidney beans, tomato sauce, chopped green pepper, instant minced onion, chili powder, and salt. Stir in uncooked noodles. Simmer the sausage-noodle mixture until the noodles are tender, 25 to 30 minutes. Makes 4 or 5 servings.

Meatballs in Onion Sauce

1 beaten egg
½ cup quick-cooking rice
¼ cup catsup
¼ cup finely chopped onion
1 tablespoon Worcestershire
    sauce
1 tablespoon snipped parsley
¾ teaspoon salt
    Dash pepper
1 pound ground beef
2 tablespoons shortening
1 10½-ounce can condensed
    onion soup
1 cup water
¼ cup cold water
3 tablespoons all-purpose flour

Advance preparation: Combine egg, uncooked rice, catsup, onion, Worcestershire sauce, parsley, salt, and pepper. Add beef; mix well. Shape into 24 meatballs. Cover; chill up to 24 hours.
Before serving: In 3-quart saucepan brown the meatballs, half at a time, in hot shortening. Drain excess fat; stir in soup and the 1 cup water. Bring to boiling; cover and simmer 20 minutes. Remove meatballs to serving bowl; keep hot. Skim excess fat from pan juices. Blend ¼ cup water slowly into flour; stir into pan juices. Cook and stir until thickened and bubbly. Pour over meatballs. Makes 6 servings.

Saucy Meatball Dinner

In saucepan combine one 8-ounce can tomato sauce; one 4-ounce can mushroom stems and pieces, drained; ¼ cup dry red wine; 1 tablespoon snipped parsley; and ¾ teaspoon dried oregano, crushed. Gently stir one 15-ounce can meatballs in gravy into the mixture.

Bring to boil; reduce heat and simmer mixture 5 minutes. Serve the meatball mixture over hot cooked noodles or spaghetti. Sprinkle with grated Parmesan cheese. Makes 4 servings.

◀ **Bring out the fondue pot** and serve your famished family *Ginger Ham Balls* and slices of *Crusty Onion Bread* (see recipe, page 20). Dunk the hot, savory ham balls in a creamy ginger sauce, a subtle flavor complement.

Mini Meat Loaves with Dill

In mixing bowl combine ¼ cup milk, ¼ cup fine dry bread crumbs, 2 tablespoons finely chopped green onion, 2 tablespoons snipped parsley, ½ teaspoon Worcestershire sauce, ½ teaspoon salt, and dash pepper. Add 1 pound ground beef and one 4½-ounce can deviled ham; mix well. Pat meat mixture into two portions, 5x5-inches each. Cut *each* square in half to form two rectangles.

Broil meat about 4 inches from heat to desired doneness, turning once. (Allow about 5 minutes on each side for medium.) Serve with Dill Sauce. Makes 4 servings.

Dill Sauce: Cook 1 tablespoon finely chopped green onion in 1 tablespoon butter *or* margarine till tender. Blend in 4 teaspoons all-purpose flour, ½ teaspoon instant beef bouillon granules, ½ teaspoon dried dillweed, ½ teaspoon paprika, and ¼ teaspoon salt. Add ½ cup milk and ½ cup water all at once. Cook; stir constantly till bubbly. Makes about 1 cup.

Ginger Ham Balls

1 beaten egg
¼ cup finely crushed cornflakes
3 tablespoons orange marmalade
1 teaspoon soy sauce
    Dash pepper
1 pound fully cooked ham, ground
½ cup mayonnaise *or*
    salad dressing
½ cup dairy sour cream
1 teaspoon lemon juice
½ teaspoon ground ginger
    Cooking oil

Advance preparation: Combine egg, cornflake crumbs, marmalade, soy sauce, and pepper. Add ham; mix well. Shape mixture into 1-inch balls, using a level tablespoonful for each ball. Refrigerate till ready to cook.
Before serving: Combine mayonnaise and sour cream. Add lemon juice and ginger; blend till smooth. Next, fill metal fondue cooker to no more than ½ capacity or to depth of 2 inches with cooking oil. Heat over range to 350°. Transfer cooker to fondue burner. Spear ham ball with fondue fork; fry till browned, about 1½ minutes. Serve with sauce. Serves 4 to 6.

Chef-Style Beef Sandwiches

2 medium onions, thinly sliced
2 tablespoons butter *or* margarine
¼ teaspoon salt
1 package refrigerated biscuits
    (10 biscuits)
1 beaten egg
Salt
10 thin slices cooked roast beef
    (about ¾ pound)
1 10-ounce package frozen
    asparagus spears, cooked
    and drained
⅔ cup dairy sour cream
1 tablespoon prepared horseradish
¾ teaspoon dillseed

Cook onions in butter till tender but not brown. Stir in the ¼ teaspoon salt. On lightly floured surface slightly overlap *two* of the biscuits. Roll out to ⅛-inch thickness, about 6 inches in length. Repeat with remaining biscuits. Place on greased baking sheet. Brush with egg. Top with onions. Bake at 475° till golden, 7 to 10 minutes.

Lightly sprinkle salt over *two* slices of roast beef; wrap around *two or three* asparagus spears. Repeat to make five rolls. Place *one* roll on each baked double biscuit. Blend sour cream, horseradish, and dillseed. Spoon about 2 tablespoons on *each* sandwich. Bake at 350° till heated through, about 10 minutes. Serves 5.

Hot Corned Beef Bunwiches

2 cups finely shredded cabbage
1 12-ounce can corned beef,
    crumbled
½ cup mayonnaise
1 teaspoon instant minced onion
1 teaspoon horseradish mustard
8 hamburger buns, split
    and buttered
16 dill pickle slices

Combine cabbage, crumbled corned beef, mayonnaise, onion, and horseradish mustard. Spread about ⅓ cup filling on bottom half of *each* hamburger bun and cover with tops. Wrap in foil. Place on baking sheet. Bake at 375° till hot, about 20 minutes. Serve 2 pickle slices with each sandwich. Serves 8.

Corn Dogs

1 cup packaged pancake mix
2 tablespoons yellow cornmeal
1 tablespoon sugar
¼ teaspoon chili powder
¼ teaspoon ground cumin
¾ cup water
8 frankfurters
Fat for frying

Combine pancake mix, cornmeal, sugar, chili powder, and cumin. Add water and beat well. Dip franks in batter and drain excess batter over bowl. In deep skillet add enough fat to make a depth of 1 inch; heat to 375°. Fry corn dogs, two at a time, for 1 to 2 minutes. Insert a wooden skewer into one end of each frank. Drain well on paper toweling. Serve hot with mustard, if desired. Makes 8 servings.

Deviled French-Fried Triangles

8 slices white bread
    Mayonnaise *or* salad dressing
1 2¼-ounce can deviled ham
4 slices sharp American cheese
    (4 ounces)
4 thin slices onion
        • • •
2 eggs
3 tablespoons dairy sour cream
    Dash salt
    Butter *or* margarine

Spread *4 slices* of the bread lightly with mayonnaise, then with deviled ham. Place a slice of cheese and a slice of onion on each. Top with remaining bread slices. Beat together eggs, sour cream, and salt. Dip each sandwich in egg mixture.

Melt butter in large skillet over medium-low heat. Fry sandwiches till cheese melts, turning to brown evenly on both sides. Cut each sandwich diagonally in half. Serves 4.

The impressive giants in front are *Laramie* ▶ *Loaves* and *Alpine Olive Sandwich* (see recipes, page 18). Trays in the middle offer *Hot Corned Beef Bunwiches* and *Chef-Style Beef Sandwiches.* The choices in the baskets are *Corn Dogs* and *Deviled French-Fried Triangles.*

Alpine Olive Sandwich

The olive-topped round loaf shown on page 17 —

- 1 cup shredded Swiss cheese
- 1 beaten egg
- 2 tablespoons chopped pimiento-stuffed green olives
- ¼ teaspoon paprika
- 1 large unsliced round loaf rye bread
- Butter *or* margarine, softened
- 4 slices bacon, crisp-cooked, drained, and crumbled
- Pimiento-stuffed green olives, sliced

Combine cheese, egg, chopped olives, and paprika. Slice rounded top off loaf. Then, cut two horizontal slices, each 1 inch thick. (Use remaining bread as desired.) Butter one side of each slice. Evenly spread *half* of the cheese filling to the edge of *each* slice. Sprinkle bacon over the tops. Place sandwiches on baking sheet. Bake at 350° till hot, 12 to 15 minutes. Garnish with sliced olives. Cut each sandwich into wedges. Serves 4 to 6.

Biscuit Burgers

- ¾ pound ground beef
- 1 teaspoon seasoned salt
- 1 package refrigerated biscuits (10 biscuits)
- Mustard
- Catsup
- Pickle relish
- 5 slices onion
- 5 slices American cheese (5 ounces)

Combine ground beef and salt; shape into five patties. In hot skillet brown the patties on both sides. On lightly floured surface roll each biscuit to a 5-inch circle. Spread *five* of the circles with mustard and catsup. Place *1* beef patty on each; top with pickle relish and *1* onion slice. Moisten edges of biscuit circles. Cover with remaining biscuits; press top and bottom edges together with a fork to seal. Prick tops. Bake on ungreased baking sheet at 375° for 15 to 17 minutes. Place *1* cheese slice on each and return to oven to melt cheese. Makes 5 sandwiches.

Laramie Loaves

Bacon identifies this sandwich shown on page 17 —

- 1 loaf French bread
- 2 cups shredded Cheddar cheese (8 ounces)
- 1 3-ounce package cream cheese, softened
- ½ cup chopped pitted ripe olives
- 6 tablespoons mayonnaise
- ¼ cup sliced green onion
- 4 teaspoons prepared mustard
- 1 teaspoon Worcestershire sauce
- 10 slices tomato
- 10 slices bacon, crisp-cooked, drained, and halved

Cut bread into top and bottom halves. Combine Cheddar cheese, cream cheese, olives, mayonnaise, onion, mustard, and Worcestershire sauce. Evenly spread *half* of the mixture on *each* half-loaf of bread. Place *five* tomato slices on top of each. Crisscross the bacon halves atop the tomatoes. Wrap each loaf loosely in foil, leaving top open. Place on baking sheets. Bake 350° for 25 to 30 minutes. Serves 10.

Hot Ham Sandwiches

Use pizza flavorings with leftover ham —

- 1¾ cups ground fully cooked ham (½ pound)
- ¾ cup shredded mozzarella cheese (3 ounces)
- ⅓ cup pizza sauce
- ¼ cup finely chopped onion
- ¼ cup chopped dill pickle
- 2 tablespoons finely chopped green pepper
- Butter *or* margarine
- 6 hamburger *or* frankfurter buns, split

Advance preparation: Combine ham, cheese, pizza sauce, onion, pickle, and green pepper. Butter buns. Assemble sandwiches, using a generous ⅓ cup filling for *each*. Bake and serve immediately or wrap in foil. Label with name and date; freeze. Serve within one month.
Before serving: Unwrap sandwiches and place on baking sheet. Bake at 350° till hot, about 45 minutes. When heating unfrozen or thawed sandwiches, allow about 20 minutes. Serves 6.

Chili Pork Sandwiches

- 8 pork cutlets (1 pound)
- 1 beaten egg
- 1 tablespoon milk
- 1 2⅜-ounce package seasoned coating mix for pork
- 8 large sesame hamburger buns, split and toasted
- 8 lettuce leaves
- 8 tomato slices
- ⅓ cup mayonnaise *or* salad dressing
- ¼ cup dairy sour cream
- 1 teaspoon chili powder

Pound pork cutlets to ¼-inch thickness. In shallow bowl combine egg and milk. Dip meat in egg mixture, then in coating mix. Place cutlets in shallow baking pan. Bake at 425° till tender, 30 to 35 minutes.

Place a cutlet on bottom half of *each* bun. Add lettuce leaf and tomato slice. Thoroughly blend mayonnaise, sour cream, and chili powder. Spoon about a tablespoonful on each sandwich; add bun tops. Makes 8 sandwiches.

Stroganoff Steakwiches

- ¼ cup butter *or* margarine
- 1 large onion, sliced and separated into rings
- ¾ cup sliced fresh mushrooms
- ¾ pound beef round steak, cut into thin strips
- 1 cup dairy sour cream
- 1 teaspoon sugar
- ½ teaspoon salt
- ½ teaspoon dry mustard
- 4 Kaiser rolls *or* hamburger buns, split, toasted, and buttered
  Paprika

Melt butter in a 10-inch skillet. Cook onion and mushrooms in butter till tender but not brown, then push to one side and add steak strips. Cook and stir over medium-high heat till browned. Blend the sour cream, sugar, salt, and dry mustard. Stir into steak and onion mixture in skillet. Heat through over low heat; *do not boil.* Spoon steak stroganoff onto the toasted and buttered rolls. Sprinkle each with paprika. Makes 4 servings.

Open-Face Sandwich Supreme

- ½ cup mayonnaise
- ½ cup catsup
- ¼ cup pickle relish
- 2 tablespoons prepared mustard
- 1 tablespoon milk
- 2 eggs
- 4 slices bacon
  Butter *or* margarine
- 4 slices rye bread
  Leaf lettuce
- 4 slices brick *or* provolone cheese (4 ounces)
- 8 thin slices cooked roast beef
  Tomato slices

Advance preparation: In a bowl combine mayonnaise, catsup, pickle relish, mustard, and milk. Cover and refrigerate. Hard-cook the eggs.
Before serving: Fry bacon till done but not crisp. Make curls by rolling each slice around tines of fork. Fasten with wooden pick. Set aside. Butter each slice of bread. Layer lettuce, cheese, roast beef, and tomato slices on top. Spoon ¼ cup dressing on *each.* Slice the hard-cooked eggs and use as garnish with bacon curls. Pass additional dressing. Serves 4.

Peachy Roast Beef Sandwiches
A calorie-counter's special —

- ¼ cup low-calorie mayonnaise-type dressing
- 1 tablespoon chili sauce
- 1 tablespoon finely chopped dill pickle
  • • •
- 4 slices Italian bread
- 4 teaspoons low-calorie mayonnaise-type dressing
- 4 lettuce leaves
- 4 thin slices cooked roast beef
- 4 juice-packed peach halves

Advance preparation: In a small bowl combine the ¼ cup mayonnaise-type dressing, chili sauce, and dill pickle. Cover and refrigerate.
Before serving: Toast bread and spread one side of each slice with 1 teaspoon mayonnaise-type dressing. Arrange one lettuce leaf, one slice roast beef, and one peach half on *each.* Drizzle dressing mixture over top. Serves 4.

Herb-Buttered Crescent Rolls

In mixing bowl cream ¼ cup softened butter *or* margarine with 1 tablespoon snipped parsley; ½ teaspoon freeze-dried chives; ¼ teaspoon dried tarragon, crushed; and ¼ teaspoon dried chervil, crushed. Separate into triangles the 8 rolls from a package of refrigerated crescent rolls. Spread each with some of the butter-herb mixture. Starting at the wide end, roll up each triangle. Place rolls, point side down, on ungreased baking sheet. Bake at 375° for 12 to 15 minutes. Makes 8 rolls.

Crusty Onion Bread

Serve with fondue, as shown on page 14 —

> ½ envelope onion soup mix
>   (¼ cup)
> 2 tablespoons shortening
> 1 tablespoon sugar
> 1 teaspoon salt
> 5½ to 6 cups all-purpose flour
> 1 package active dry yeast
>   Cornmeal
> 1 slightly beaten egg white

In saucepan combine 2¼ cups water with dry soup mix; cover and simmer 10 minutes. Stir in shortening, sugar, and salt. Cool till lukewarm. In a large mixing bowl combine 2½ cups of the flour with yeast. Add onion mixture. Beat at low speed of electric mixer for ½ minute, scraping bowl. Beat at high speed for 3 minutes. By hand, stir in enough remaining flour to make a moderately stiff dough. Knead on floured surface till smooth (8 to 10 minutes). Shape into ball. Place in greased bowl; turn once. Cover; let rise in warm place till double (about 1 hour).

Punch down dough. Turn out on lightly floured surface; divide in half. Cover and let rest 10 minutes. Shape into two 12-inch loaves; taper ends. Place each on a greased baking sheet sprinkled with cornmeal. With a sharp knife, make diagonal cuts 2½ inches apart and ¼ inch deep on tops of loaves. Cover and let rise till double (about 30 minutes).

Bake at 375° for 20 minutes. Brush loaves with mixture of beaten egg white and 1 tablespoon water. Bake 10 minutes longer. Remove from baking sheets; cool. Makes 2 loaves.

ABC Sandwich

Avocado, bacon, and crab are the filling —

> ⅓ cup mayonnaise *or*
>   salad dressing
> 2 tablespoons dairy sour cream
> 1 tablespoon lemon juice
> 8 slices bacon, crisp-cooked,
>   drained, and crumbled
> ¼ cup finely chopped celery
> ¼ cup finely chopped radish
> 1 7½-ounce can crab meat, drained,
>   flaked, and cartilage removed
> 1 avocado, seeded, peeled, and
>   finely chopped or mashed
> ¼ teaspoon salt
> 1 loaf Quick Rye Bread (see
>   recipe below) *or* 1 unsliced
>   round loaf rye bread
>   Butter *or* margarine
>   Lettuce leaves
> 6 cherry tomatoes

Blend mayonnaise, sour cream, and lemon juice. To *half* the mixture stir in bacon, celery, and radish. To remaining mixture stir in crab meat, avocado, and salt. Cut bread into three crosswise slices. Toast cut surfaces under broiler; spread with butter. Spread bottom slice with bacon mixture. Top with some lettuce and middle slice of bread. Spread with crab mixture; add lettuce. Top with remaining slice of bread. Insert skewers through tomatoes and into loaf from top to bottom. Cut into wedges. Serves 6.

Quick Rye Bread

Remove yeast packet from one 13¾-ounce package hot roll mix. In large mixing bowl dissolve yeast in ¾ cup *warm* milk (110°). Stir in 1 egg and ¼ cup molasses. Combine the flour from hot roll mix with ¾ cup rye flour. Stir in 2 teaspoons caraway seed and ½ teaspoon salt. Add to yeast mixture; blend well.

Turn dough out on a lightly floured surface and knead till smooth (12 to 15 strokes). Shape into two balls. Place each on a greased baking sheet and flatten to a 5-inch diameter. Cover and let rise in a warm place till double (about 1 hour). Bake at 350° till done, about 25 minutes. Remove from baking sheets and cool on wire racks. Makes 2 loaves.

ABC Sandwich features avocado, bacon, and crab meat fillings spread on thick slices of rye bread, then skewered and cut into 6 wedges.

Round loaves of homemade *Quick Rye Bread* can be used for the sandwich. Just add rye flour, molasses, and caraway seed to a hot roll mix.

Onion-Cheese Bread

   1 beaten egg
  ½ cup milk
 1½ cups packaged biscuit mix
   2 tablespoons grated Parmesan
     cheese
   2 tablespoons snipped
     parsley
   2 teaspoons onion dip mix
     Grated Parmesan cheese

Combine beaten egg and milk. Add to biscuit mix, stirring only till all is moistened. Blend in 2 tablespoons grated Parmesan cheese, parsley, and dry onion dip mix. Spread dough in greased 8x1½-inch round baking pan.

   Sprinkle Parmesan cheese over top. Bake at 400° till wooden pick comes out clean, 15 to 20 minutes. Serve warm. Makes 6 to 8 wedges.

Hot Cheese Loaf

   2 loaves brown-and-serve bread
     with pull-apart slices
   1 4-ounce container whipped
     cream cheese with bacon
     and horseradish
   1 teaspoon prepared mustard
   1 teaspoon finely chopped
     green onion

Bake bread according to package directions. Thoroughly blend together the cream cheese, mustard, and onion. Partially split the warm bread along marked separations, leaving slices attached at the bottom. Spread some cheese mixture between every other slice. Serve immediately. (To reheat, wrap in foil and bake at 375° till heated through, 12 to 15 minutes.) Makes 14 to 16 slices.

Broccoli-Corn Bake

    1 tablespoon instant minced onion
    1 16-ounce can cream-style corn
    1 10-ounce package frozen chopped
        broccoli, cooked and drained
    1 beaten egg
    ¼ cup coarsely crushed saltine
        crackers (6 crackers)
    2 tablespoons butter *or*
        margarine, melted
    ¼ teaspoon salt
        Dash pepper
    ¼ cup coarsely crushed saltine
        crackers (6 crackers)
    1 tablespoon butter *or*
        margarine, melted

Advance preparation: Soak onion in 2 table-spoons water for 2 to 3 minutes; drain. Blend corn, broccoli, egg, ¼ cup crumbs, onion, 2 tablespoons butter, salt, and pepper. Turn into 1-quart casserole. Cover and refrigerate.
Before serving: Uncover casserole. Mix ¼ cup cracker crumbs with 1 tablespoon melted butter. Sprinkle over vegetables. Bake at 350° for 1 hour and 10 minutes. (If baked immediately after preparation, reduce baking time to 45 to 50 minutes.) Makes 6 servings.

Eggplant Patties

    1 medium eggplant, peeled
        and cubed
    1¼ cups coarsely crushed rich
        round crackers (20 crackers)
    1¼ cups shredded sharp
        American cheese (5 ounces)
    2 beaten eggs
    2 tablespoons snipped parsley
    2 tablespoons sliced green onion
    1 clove garlic, minced
    ½ teaspoon salt
    ⅛ teaspoon pepper
    2 tablespoons cooking oil

In saucepan add eggplant to small amount of boiling water. Cover; cook till tender, about 5 minutes. Drain very well and mash. Mix with crumbs, cheese, eggs, parsley, onion, garlic, salt, and pepper. Shape into eight 3-inch patties. In skillet heat oil. Cook patties till golden, about 3 minutes per side. Serves 4.

Creamy Dilled Corn
Ripe olives and dillweed spark canned corn—

    2 tablespoons butter *or*
        margarine
    ½ cup chopped celery
    ½ cup chopped onion
    1 17-ounce can cream-style corn
    ¼ cup sliced pitted
        ripe olives
    ¼ teaspoon dried dillweed
        Paprika

In medium saucepan melt butter. Add celery and onion. Cover and cook till vegetables are tender, about 10 minutes. Stir in corn, olives, and dillweed. Heat through. Turn into serving bowl. Sprinkle with paprika. Serves 4 or 5.

Creamed Peas and Mushrooms

    1 10-ounce package frozen
        peas with sliced mushrooms
    1 3-ounce package cream cheese
        with chives, cut in cubes
    2 tablespoons milk

In saucepan cook peas and mushrooms according to package directions; do not drain. Add cream cheese cubes. Cover and cook over low heat till cheese is softened, about 2 minutes. Add milk; stir gently till sauce is smooth and blended. Heat through. Makes 4 servings.

Chinese Spinach
Water chestnuts for crunch, soy sauce for taste—

    1 pound fresh spinach
    2 tablespoons cooking oil
    2 tablespoons soy sauce
    ½ teaspoon sugar
    2 tablespoons finely chopped
        onion
    1 5-ounce can water chestnuts

Wash spinach and pat dry. Remove stems and cut into 1-inch pieces. Tear leaves into bite-size pieces. In large saucepan simmer spinach in small amount of water for 3 minutes. Drain thoroughly. In skillet heat oil, soy, and sugar; add spinach and onion. Cook, tossing till spinach is well-coated, 2 to 3 minutes. Stir in water chestnuts. Makes 4 servings.

French-Style Baked Tomatoes

6 medium tomatoes
¼ cup cooking oil
4 teaspoons vinegar
1 tablespoon sugar
1½ teaspoons instant minced onion
¼ teaspoon salt
¼ teaspoon dry mustard
¼ teaspoon Worcestershire sauce
• • •
½ cup crushed saltine
    crackers (about 14 crackers)
1 tablespoon butter *or*
    margarine, melted
Snipped parsley

Cut thin slice from top of each tomato. Hollow tomatoes out slightly. Combine oil, vinegar, sugar, onion, salt, mustard, and Worcestershire sauce. Spoon some of mixture into center of each tomato. Combine cracker crumbs and butter; sprinkle over tops.

Place tomatoes in shallow baking dish. Bake at 350° till tomatoes are done, 25 to 30 minutes. Garnish by sprinkling snipped parsley over each tomato. Makes 6 servings.

Cheesy Potato Sticks

Kids of all ages will like these —

2 tablespoons butter *or* margarine
2 tablespoons all-purpose flour
¼ teaspoon salt
    Dash pepper
1 cup milk
1 cup shredded sharp
    American cheese (4 ounces)
1 tablespoon chopped canned
    pimiento
1 16-ounce package frozen
    french-fried potatoes

In saucepan melt butter over low heat. Blend in flour, salt, and pepper. Add milk all at once. Cook quickly, stirring constantly, till thickened and bubbly. Add *half* of the shredded cheese. Stir till cheese melts; stir in pimiento. Place potatoes in a 10x6x2-inch baking dish. Pour cheese sauce over potatoes. Sprinkle with the remaining shredded cheese. Cover and bake at 350° for 15 minutes. Uncover and bake 25 minutes more. Serves 4.

Zucchini Sweet-Sour Medley

2 tablespoons cooking oil
4 teaspoons cornstarch
1 tablespoon sugar
1 tablespoon instant minced onion
2 teaspoons prepared mustard
¾ teaspoon salt
½ teaspoon garlic salt
    Dash pepper
½ cup water
¼ cup vinegar
4 cups bias-sliced zucchini
    (3 or 4 zucchini)
1 cup bias-sliced celery
2 tomatoes, quartered

In medium skillet combine oil, cornstarch, sugar, onion, prepared mustard, salt, garlic salt, and pepper. Add water and vinegar; cook and stir till mixture thickens and bubbles.

Add zucchini and celery. Cover and cook till vegetables are crisp-tender, 7 to 8 minutes; stir occasionally. Add tomatoes; cover and cook the vegetable mixture till heated through, 2 to 3 minutes more. Makes 6 servings.

Vegetable Potpourri

2 strips bacon, chopped
¾ cup chopped onion
3 medium ears fresh corn, rinsed,
    or 1 10-ounce package frozen
    whole kernel corn
4 medium zucchini, sliced
    (1½ pounds)
1½ teaspoons ground cumin
½ teaspoon salt
⅛ teaspoon garlic powder
3 medium tomatoes, peeled
    and cut in wedges
½ cup shredded American cheese
    (2 ounces)

In large skillet cook bacon till crisp. Add onion; cook till tender but not brown. Cut off tips of kernels from ears of corn; scrape cobs with dull edge of knife. Add corn and scrapings to skillet with zucchini, cumin, salt, and garlic powder. Cover and cook till zucchini is tender, 15 to 20 minutes. Add tomatoes; heat through. Spoon into serving dish and sprinkle with shredded cheese. Serves 8.

Bean and Potato Salad

1 9-ounce package frozen
   Italian green beans
1 16-ounce can sliced potatoes,
   drained
1 tablespoon sliced green onion
¼ cup herb and garlic French
   salad dressing
¼ cup dairy sour cream
¼ cup mayonnaise
¼ teaspoon celery seed
⅛ teaspoon salt
   Lettuce cups
   Sliced radishes

Advance preparation: Cook beans according to package directions; drain. Combine beans, potatoes, and onion. Pour dressing over all, tossing lightly. Cover; refrigerate 2 to 12 hours, stirring occasionally.
Before serving: Combine sour cream, mayonnaise, celery seed, and salt. Add to vegetables. Stir lightly to mix. Mound in lettuce cups; garnish with radish slices. Serves 4 to 6.

South Sea Salad

1 avocado, halved and seeded
   Dill pickle juice
½ cup mayonnaise
½ cup dairy sour cream
¼ cup dill pickle juice
1 tablespoon snipped parsley
2 teaspoons snipped chives
1 teaspoon dried dillweed
6 cups torn lettuce
1 11-ounce can mandarin orange
   sections, chilled and drained
1 cup sliced fresh mushrooms
1 small onion, sliced and
   separated into rings
1 green pepper, sliced in rings

Brush cut surface of half the avocado with pickle juice; refrigerate. Peel and mash remaining half; blend with mayonnaise, sour cream, ¼ cup pickle juice, parsley, chives, and dillweed. Cover and chill. Place lettuce in salad bowl. Peel and slice reserved avocado. Arrange atop lettuce with oranges, mushrooms, onion, and green pepper. Toss with desired amount of dressing. Serves 4 to 6.

Easy Apricot Salad

Drain one 8¼-ounce can seedless grapes, reserving syrup. Soften one 3-ounce package cream cheese; blend with ¼ cup sugar and ¼ cup mayonnaise. Stir in one 21-ounce can apricot pie filling, 1 cup tiny marshmallows, 1 cup chopped apple, and grapes. Thin with 1 or 2 tablespoons reserved grape syrup. Chill well. Spoon salad into lettuce cups. Serves 10.

Rosé Fruit Mold

2 envelopes unflavored gelatin
⅓ cup sugar
1 16-ounce can grapefruit
   sections
1 cup rosé wine
2 tablespoons lemon juice
3 drops red food coloring
1 cup seedless green grapes
   Celery Seed Dressing

In saucepan soften gelatin in 1½ cups cold water; stir in sugar and ¼ teaspoon salt. Stir over low heat till gelatin dissolves. Drain grapefruit, reserving ½ cup syrup. Stir syrup, wine, lemon juice, and food coloring into gelatin. Chill till partially set. Halve grapes; fold into salad with grapefruit. Turn into 5½-cup ring mold. Chill till firm. Unmold and serve with Celery Seed Dressing. Serves 6 to 8.

Celery Seed Dressing: In bowl combine ½ cup sugar, ⅓ cup lemon juice, 1 teaspoon celery seed, 1 teaspoon dry mustard, 1 teaspoon paprika, and ½ teaspoon salt. Slowly add ¾ cup salad oil, beating with electric mixer or rotary beater till thickened. Makes 1⅓ cups.

Jiffy Coleslaw Salad

Core 1 small head cabbage; cut in wedges. Slice 3 stalks celery. Cut ½ green pepper in pieces. Place ⅓ of the vegetables in blender container with 1 thin slice onion. Add cold water to cover. Blend a few seconds till coarsely chopped. Remove; drain well. Repeat with remaining vegetables; drain. Combine ¾ cup coleslaw salad dressing, ½ teaspoon celery seed, and ¼ teaspoon salt. Toss dressing with vegetables. Makes 6 servings.

Lemon Cheesecake Pudding is a refreshingly tart dessert choice for people on the go. Individual servings are made ahead, ready for serving. Lemon yogurt contributes to the flavor, along with fresh lemon juice and grated peel. It's a creamy-rich pudding with light, fluffy texture.

Wilted Lettuce-Orange Salad

   3 slices bacon
 ¼ cup vinegar
   1 tablespoon salad oil
   2 teaspoons sugar
 ¼ teaspoon salt
 ⅛ teaspoon dried tarragon,
      crushed
      Dash freshly ground pepper
 ¼ cup chopped celery
   1 tablespoon sliced green onion
   1 medium head lettuce, torn
      (6 cups)
   2 medium oranges, peeled and
      sectioned

In large skillet cook bacon till crisp; drain, reserving 2 tablespoons drippings in skillet. Crumble bacon; set aside. Stir vinegar, oil, sugar, and seasonings into drippings in skillet; bring to boiling. Add celery and onion. Gradually add torn lettuce, tossing just till leaves are coated with dressing mixture and wilted slightly. Add orange sections and bacon. Toss lightly; serve immediately. Serves 8 to 10.

Lemon Cheesecake Pudding

 ¼ cup sugar
   1 teaspoon unflavored gelatin
 ¼ teaspoon salt
   2 3-ounce packages cream cheese,
      softened
 ½ cup lemon yogurt
 ¼ teaspoon grated lemon peel
   1 tablespoon lemon juice
      Few drops yellow food coloring
 ½ cup frozen whipped dessert
      topping, thawed
   1 teaspoon finely crushed
      graham crackers
      Lemon peel twists

In small saucepan combine sugar, gelatin, and salt; add ⅔ cup cold water. Stir over low heat till gelatin dissolves. Remove from heat. Add cream cheese, yogurt, lemon peel, lemon juice, and food coloring; beat till smooth. Fold in the whipped topping. Pour into four ½-cup dishes. Sprinkle with crushed crackers. Chill till firm, 4 to 5 hours. Garnish with lemon peel twists. Makes 4 servings.

Fudge Nut Angel Cake

Cut cake center in squares; serve as shortcake—

        1 package chocolate fudge
           frosting mix
           (for 2-layer cake)
        2 cups whipping cream
        1 8- or 9-inch sponge *or*
           angel cake
        1 medium banana, sliced (1 cup)
        ½ cup chopped walnuts

Combine frosting mix and whipping cream. Cover and chill 1 hour. Cut a 1-inch slice from top of cake; set aside. With knife parallel to cake sides, cut around cake 1 inch from center hole and 1 inch from outer edge, leaving cake walls 1 inch thick. Remove center with fork, leaving 1-inch-thick base. Place base on plate.

Beat frosting mixture till soft peaks form. Fold banana into *1 cup* of mixture; fill cake. Replace top slice of cake. Frost with remaining whipped mixture. Garnish with nuts. Chill 2 to 3 hours. Slice with serrated or electric knife. Makes 12 to 16 servings.

Pumpkin-Rum Cake

        2 packages pound cake mix
        1 16-ounce can pumpkin
     1½ teaspoons pumpkin pie spice
        1 cup sugar
        1 cup orange juice
        2 inches stick cinnamon
        ¼ cup rum

Combine cake mixes and prepare together according to package directions, *except* decrease water to a total of ⅔ cup. Stir in pumpkin and pie spice. Turn into well-greased and floured 10-inch fluted tube pan. Bake at 325° till cake tests done, about 1 hour and 20 minutes.

Cool in pan 10 minutes. Remove to wire rack and cool 20 minutes more. Place on serving plate. Using long-tined fork or skewer, punch holes in top of cake at 1-inch intervals.

In saucepan prepare syrup by combining sugar, orange juice, and cinnamon. Bring to boiling. Remove cinnamon; stir in rum. Spoon syrup very slowly over cake, a small amount at a time, allowing cake to absorb syrup. Spoon any syrup that runs onto plate back over cake. Chill till serving time. Makes 12 to 16 servings.

Coconut-Orange Cake

Save egg yolks for Custard Sauce recipe below—

        1 package 2-layer-size
           white cake mix
        1 cup milk
        2 egg whites
        ½ of a 6-ounce can frozen
           orange juice concentrate,
           thawed (⅓ cup)
        ½ cup flaked coconut
        1 cup sugar
        ⅓ cup water
        ¼ teaspoon cream of tartar
           Dash salt
        2 egg whites
        1 teaspoon vanilla

In mixing bowl combine cake mix, milk, 2 egg whites, and orange juice concentrate. Beat 4 minutes at medium speed of electric mixer, scraping the sides of bowl often. Fold in flaked coconut. Pour into 2 greased and floured 9x1½-inch round baking pans. Bake at 350° for 18 to 20 minutes. Cool in pan 10 minutes; remove to wire rack and cool.

In saucepan prepare syrup by combining sugar, water, cream of tartar, and salt. Bring to boiling; stir till sugar dissolves. In small mixing bowl slowly add syrup to 2 unbeaten egg whites. Beat till stiff peaks form, about 5 minutes. Beat in vanilla.

Assemble cake on serving plate, spooning some frosting between the two layers. Spread remaining on top and sides of cake. If desired, decorate cake with tinted coconut.

Custard Sauce

        4 beaten egg yolks
        ¼ cup sugar
           Dash salt
        2 cups milk, scalded and
           slightly cooled
        1 teaspoon vanilla

In heavy saucepan mix egg yolks, sugar, and salt. Gradually stir in milk. Cook and stir over low heat till mixture coats metal spoon. Remove from heat. Cool pan at once by setting in cold water. Stir 1 to 2 minutes, then stir in vanilla. Chill. Serve over fruit, baked puddings, or soufflés. Makes 2 cups.

Pinwheel Peach Cobbler

> ½ cup packaged biscuit mix
> 2 tablespoons finely chopped
>   pecans
> 1 tablespoon sugar
> 2 tablespoons milk
> 1 teaspoon cooking oil
> 1 tablespoon strawberry preserves
> 1 16-ounce can peach slices
> ¼ cup sugar
> 2 teaspoons cornstarch
> 2 teaspoons lemon juice
> 1 tablespoon butter *or* margarine

Combine biscuit mix, pecans, and 1 tablespoon sugar; add milk and oil. Mix well. On well-floured surface pat dough to a 6x4-inch rectangle; spread with preserves. Roll up from short side; cut into 4 slices. Drain peaches, reserving syrup; add water to make 1 cup. In saucepan combine ¼ cup sugar, cornstarch, and dash salt; stir in syrup and lemon juice. Cook and stir till bubbly. Add butter and peaches; heat through. Spoon into four 1-cup baking dishes. Place biscuit atop each. Bake at 425° for 15 minutes. Serves 4.

Quick Cherry Cream Tarts

> Pastry for 2-crust 9-inch pie
> 1 cup milk
> 1 cup dairy sour cream
> ¼ teaspoon almond extract
> 1 3⅝- or 3 ¾-ounce package
>   *instant* vanilla pudding mix
> 1 21-ounce can cherry pie
>   filling (2 cups)
> 2 tablespoons slivered almonds,
>   toasted

Prepare pastry. On floured surface roll pastry ⅛ inch thick. Cut eight 5-inch circles. Fit over inverted muffin pans or custard cups, pinching together at 4 corners; prick with fork. Bake at 450° till golden, 9 to 10 minutes. Cool. In mixing bowl combine milk, sour cream, and almond extract. Add pudding mix; beat with electric mixer or rotary beater till creamy and well blended, about 2 minutes. Spoon into tart shells. Top with cherry pie filling. Add a dollop of additional sour cream, if desired. Sprinkle with almonds. Chill. Serves 8.

Easy-As-Pie Parfaits

Thaw one 17½-ounce carton frozen vanilla pudding *or* open one 18-ounce can vanilla pudding. Blend with 1 cup dairy sour cream. In six parfait glasses spoon alternate layers of pudding mixture with contents of one 21-ounce can fruit pie filling (apricot, cherry, peach, or blueberry). Refrigerate till serving time. Serves 6.

Harvey Wallbanger Sherbet

> 2 cups milk
> 1 cup sugar
> 1 cup light cream
> 1 cup orange juice
> 3 tablespoons vodka
> 3 tablespoons Galliano
> 2 tablespoons lemon juice

In saucepan heat *1 cup* of the milk; add sugar and stir till dissolved. Stir in the remaining milk, cream, orange juice, vodka, Galliano, lemon juice, and dash salt; mix well. Freeze in ice cream freezer according to manufacturer's directions. Let ripen 1 hour for a soft spoonable texture. For firmer scoops, pack sherbet into carton, cover, and place in freezer 1 to 2 hours. Makes about 3 pints.

Mandarin-Raisin Dessert Sauce

Spoon warm sauce over ice cream or cake slices—

> 1 11-ounce can mandarin orange
>   sections
> ⅔ cup orange juice
> ½ cup light raisins
> 2 tablespoons packed brown sugar
> 1 tablespoon cornstarch
> ⅛ teaspoon ground cloves
> ¼ cup orange liqueur
> 1 tablespoon butter *or*
>   margarine

Drain oranges, reserving ⅓ cup syrup; pour into saucepan. Add orange juice and raisins. Bring to boiling. Remove from heat; cover and let stand till cool, 15 to 20 minutes. Combine brown sugar, cornstarch, and cloves; add to raisin mixture. Cook and stir till thickened and bubbly. Stir in orange liqueur and butter. Add oranges; heat through. Makes about 2 cups.

Meals for the Outdoors

You don't have to live near the ocean to enjoy this elegant picnic. Regardless of where you are, Lemon-Marinated Salmon Steaks, Vegetable Salad Rolls, and icy-cold watermelon are a hard-to-beat combination. (See index for recipe pages.)

Menus for Outdoor Eating

BACKYARD COOKOUT

Fish House Barbecue
Roasted Corn on the Cob
Carrot Sticks   Radish Roses
Hurry-Up Cheese Buns
Cookies
Iced Tea   Beer

Special Helps: Plan a backyard feast and invite some friends over to enjoy the barbecue. Bake the cheese buns and clean all the vegetables early in the day. After that's done, assemble the ingredients for the barbecue sauce and you're all set! Just before your guests arrive, start the charcoal.

Fish House Barbecue

    1 15-ounce can tomato sauce
    ½ cup dry red wine
    ½ cup butter *or* margarine
    2 tablespoons lemon juice
    2 tablespoons chopped
        green onion
    1 teaspoon sugar
    1 teaspoon dried salad herbs
    ½ teaspoon salt
      Few drops bottled hot
        pepper sauce
          • • •
    6 whole pan-dressed brook *or*
        lake trout *or* perch
        (about ½ pound each)

In small heavy saucepan combine all ingredients except fish. Simmer, uncovered, over coals 10 to 15 minutes. Meanwhile, grill fish over *hot* coals 10 to 12 minutes on each side. Brush both sides of fish with sauce during last few minutes of grilling. Pass the sauce. Serves 6.

Roasted Corn on the Cob

    ½ cup butter *or* margarine,
        softened
    1 teaspoon salt
    ½ teaspoon dried rosemary,
        crushed
    ½ teaspoon dried marjoram,
        crushed
    6 ears corn

Cream together butter and salt till fluffy. Combine herbs and blend into butter. Keep butter at room temperature for 1 hour to mellow. Turn back husks of corn; remove silk with stiff brush. Place each ear on a piece of heavy foil. Spread corn with about *1 tablespoon* of the butter. Lay husks back in position. Wrap corn securely. Roast ears directly on *hot* coals; turn frequently till corn is tender, 12 to 15 minutes. Or, if you have a covered grill with an elevated rack, roast corn according to manufacturer's directions. Serves 6.

Hurry-Up Cheese Buns

In mixer bowl combine 1 cup all-purpose flour and 1 package active dry yeast. Heat one 5-ounce jar sharp American cheese spread, ½ cup water, ¼ cup shortening, 2 tablespoons sugar, and 1 teaspoon salt just till warm (115-120°), stirring constantly. Add to dry mixture; add 1 egg. Beat at low speed of electric mixer for ½ minute, scraping bowl. Beat 3 minutes at high speed. By hand, stir in 1 cup all-purpose flour. Turn out onto floured surface. Shape into 12 rolls; place in well-greased muffin pans. Let rise till nearly double (1 to 1½ hours). Bake at 350° for 15 to 18 minutes. Remove from pans; cool. Makes 12.

Food cooked outdoors just tastes better—so try *Fish House Barbecue*. Quickly grill the fish over the hot coals and baste with a mellow wine-flavored barbecue sauce. *Roasted Corn on the Cob* makes a tasty accompaniment.

TAKE-ALONG PICNIC

Crisp Chive Chicken
Potato Chips
Marinated Three-Bean Salad
Dill Pickles   Ripe Olives
Rye Bread   Butter
Choco-Oatmeal Cake
Lemonade   Coffee

Special Helps: Lugging the grill and charcoal around is a less-than-desirable aspect of having a picnic. But with these foods you can forget all that. They are ready-to-eat when you leave the house. Simply pack the chicken, salad, relishes, and lemonade separately in leakproof food containers with snap-tight lids, and carry the food in an ice chest filled with blocks of ice.

Marinated Three-Bean Salad

    1 8½-ounce can lima beans,
       drained
    1 8-ounce can cut green beans,
       drained
    1 8-ounce can red kidney
       beans, drained
    1 medium sweet onion, sliced
       and separated into rings
       (½ cup)
    ½ cup chopped green pepper
       • • •
    ⅔ cup vinegar
    ½ cup salad oil
    ¼ cup sugar
    1 teaspoon celery seed

In large bowl combine the lima beans, green beans, red kidney beans, onion rings, and chopped green pepper. In a screw-top jar combine vinegar, salad oil, sugar, and celery seed; shake to mix well. Pour the marinade over the vegetables and stir lightly. Cover and chill 8 hours or overnight, stirring frequently. Drain before serving. Makes 8 servings.

Crisp Chive Chicken

    1 cup finely crushed cornflakes
       (2 cups cornflakes)
    ⅓ cup freeze-dried chives
    1 teaspoon salt
    ¼ teaspoon garlic powder
    ¼ teaspoon pepper
    1 2½- to 3-pound ready-to-cook
       broiler-fryer chicken, cut up
    ⅓ cup evaporated milk

Combine crumbs, chives, salt, garlic powder, and pepper. Dip chicken pieces in evaporated milk, then roll them in cornflake mixture. Place chicken, skin side up, in 15½x10½x1-inch baking pan. Bake at 350° for 1 hour. Remove from oven. Wrap and chill thoroughly. Serves 4.

Choco-Oatmeal Cake

    1¼ cups boiling water
    1 cup quick-cooking rolled oats
    ½ cup butter or margarine
    1 4-ounce package sweet cooking
       chocolate, broken up
    1½ cups all-purpose flour
    1 cup granulated sugar
    1 teaspoon baking soda
    ½ teaspoon salt
    1 cup packed brown sugar
    3 eggs
    Caramel-Nut Topping

In medium mixing bowl pour boiling water over oats; add butter and chocolate. Let stand 20 minutes; stir till well combined.

In large mixing bowl thoroughly stir together flour, granulated sugar, soda, and salt. Stir in brown sugar. Add eggs and oat mixture. Beat at low speed of electric mixer till thoroughly combined. Scrape sides of bowl. Turn into greased and floured 13x9x2-inch baking pan. Bake at 350° till done, 35 to 40 minutes.

Spread Caramel-Nut Topping over hot cake. Broil 4 to 5 inches from heat till bubbly, about 1 minute. Serve warm or cool.

Caramel-Nut Topping: In small saucepan cook and stir ¾ cup packed brown sugar, 6 tablespoons butter or margarine, and ¼ cup light cream till mixture comes to boil; reduce heat. Simmer till thick, 2 to 3 minutes, stirring often. Stir in ½ cup chopped pecans.

MAKE-AHEAD PICNIC

(See photo, page 28)

Lemon-Marinated Salmon Steaks
Vegetable Salad Rolls
Watermelon
or
Brandy Alexander Brownies
Wine   Iced Tea

Special Helps: The evening before the picnic, prepare the salmon steaks and vegetable salad. Chill them in the refrigerator along with the watermelon. Keep the cold foods cold by packing the lunch in an ice chest. When you arrive at your picnic site, simply assemble the rolls and enjoy the outing.

Brandy Alexander Brownies

    6 tablespoons butter, softened
    ¾ cup sugar
    2 eggs
    1 1-ounce square unsweetened
        chocolate, melted and cooled
    2 tablespoons crème de cacao
    2 tablespoons brandy
    ⅔ cup all-purpose flour
    ½ teaspoon baking powder
    ⅓ cup chopped nuts
      Sweet Brandy Frosting

In mixing bowl cream together the butter and sugar till fluffy. Add eggs; beat well. Blend in the cooled chocolate, crème de cacao, and brandy. Stir together the flour, baking powder, and ¼ teaspoon salt. Stir into creamed mixture. Stir in the chopped nuts. Spread in a greased 9x9x2-inch baking pan. Bake at 350° for 20 to 25 minutes. Cool. Frost with Sweet Brandy Frosting. Cut into bars. Makes 24.

Sweet Brandy Frosting: Cream together 2 tablespoons softened butter *or* margarine and 1 cup sifted powdered sugar. Blend in 1 tablespoon crème de cacao and 1 tablespoon brandy to make of spreading consistency.

Vegetable Salad Rolls

    ½ cup chopped green pepper
    ½ cup chopped seeded cucumber
    ½ cup chopped seeded tomato
    ½ cup chopped celery
    2 tablespoons chopped red onion
    2 tablespoons snipped parsley
    2 tablespoons chopped dill pickle
    ⅓ cup sour cream dip with garlic
    ¼ cup mayonnaise *or* salad
        dressing
    ¼ teaspoon salt
    6 hard rolls

Combine green pepper, cucumber, tomato, celery, onion, parsley, and dill pickle. Combine sour cream dip, mayonnaise, and salt; gently fold into vegetables. Cover and chill till serving time. Split rolls and scoop out the centers; wrap. Just before serving, fill rolls with chilled salad mixture. Makes 6 servings.

Lemon-Marinated Salmon Steaks

    6 fresh *or* frozen salmon steaks
    ½ cup lemon juice
    ⅓ cup sliced green onion
    ¼ cup cooking oil
    3 tablespoons snipped parsley
    3 tablespoons finely chopped
        green pepper
    1 tablespoon sugar
    2 teaspoons dry mustard
    ¾ teaspoon salt
    ⅛ teaspoon cayenne
      Lemon wedges

Thaw salmon steaks, if frozen. Bring 1 cup water to boiling in 10-inch skillet or fish poacher with tight-fitting cover. Sprinkle salmon with a little salt. Place *half* of the fish on greased rack in pan so fish does not touch water. Cover pan tightly and steam till fish flakes easily when tested with a fork, 5 to 7 minutes. Carefully remove fish to shallow dish. Repeat with remaining fish. In screwtop jar combine remaining ingredients except lemon wedges; shake vigorously to blend. Pour over salmon steaks. Cover and chill 2 hours, spooning marinade over steaks several times. Drain before serving and spoon vegetables over top. Serve with lemon wedges. Serves 6.

Good Eating Outdoors

Chuckwagon Chowder

> 2 11-ounce cans condensed
>   chili beef soup
> 1 11-ounce can condensed Cheddar
>   cheese soup
> 1 16-ounce can lima beans
> 1 teaspoon instant minced onion
> ¼ teaspoon dried thyme, crushed

In 3-quart saucepan combine soups, undrained beans, onion, thyme, and 1 soup can water (1¼ cups). Bring to boiling over medium heat, stirring occasionally. Reduce heat; simmer and stir 5 minutes. Makes 8 cups.

Frank and Bean Skillet

> 1 envelope sour cream sauce mix
> ¾ cup milk
>   Few drops bottled hot pepper
>   sauce
> 1 22-ounce jar baked beans
> 4 or 5 frankfurters, bias-sliced
> 1 3½-ounce can French-fried
>   onions

In skillet blend together sauce mix, milk, and pepper sauce. Stir in beans and franks. Cook over *medium* coals, stirring occasionally, till mixture is heated through. Before serving, stir in about ¾ of the onions. Sprinkle remaining onions atop each serving. Serves 4.

Super-Simple Skillet Supper

In skillet combine one 5½-ounce package dry hashed brown potatoes with onion; one 16-ounce can cut green beans, undrained; one 12-ounce can luncheon meat, cut in strips; 1½ cups water; one 5⅓-ounce can evaporated milk; one 5-ounce jar cheese spread with hickory smoke flavor; and dash pepper. Cover and cook over medium heat, stirring occasionally. Heat till mixture is bubbly and potatoes are tender, about 10 minutes. Trim with additional luncheon meat strips, if desired. Serves 4.

Sunny Ham-Burgers

Beef and ham with a sunflower seed filling—

> 1 beaten egg
> 2 tablespoons milk
> ½ cup whole wheat bread crumbs
> ½ pound ground fully cooked ham
> ½ pound ground beef
> ¼ cup shelled sunflower seeds
> ¼ cup chopped onion
> 2 teaspoons milk
> 5 whole wheat hamburger buns,
>   split and toasted
>   Prepared horseradish

Combine egg, 2 tablespoons milk, crumbs, and dash pepper. Add ground meats; mix well. Using about ¼ cup mixture for each patty, shape meat mixture into ten 3½-inch patties; set aside. Combine sunflower seeds, onion, and 2 teaspoons milk. Spoon 1 heaping tablespoon of the mixture onto center of *five* patties. Top with remaining five patties. Press edges together well to seal. Broil over *hot* coals for 12 to 15 minutes, turning once. (Centers will remain pink due to ham). Serve on buns with horseradish. Serves 5.

Burger Dogs

In mixing bowl combine 1 beaten egg, ¼ cup milk, ¾ cup soft bread crumbs, 2 tablespoons chopped onion, ½ teaspoon salt, and dash pepper. Thoroughly mix in 1 pound ground beef. Divide into 6 equal portions; roll flat between pieces of waxed paper. Shape around 6 frankfurters, covering each completely. Chill. Brush burgers with Barbecue Sauce. Using 6 slices bacon, wrap one slice around each burger; secure with wooden picks. Grill meat over *hot* coals about 15 minutes, turning as needed to cook evenly. Brush sauce over meat; place in split and toasted frankfurter buns. Pass remaining sauce. Serves 6.

Barbecue Sauce: In saucepan combine 1 cup catsup; ¼ cup butter, melted; ¼ cup molasses; and 2 tablespoons vinegar. Blend thoroughly and simmer 15 minutes. Reheat before serving.

Burrito Burgers

        1 cup refried beans
            (½ of 15-ounce can)
        1 4-ounce can mild green chili
            peppers, drained and chopped
        ¼ cup chopped onion
        ¾ teaspoon salt
        1½ pounds ground beef
        4 slices sharp American cheese,
            cut in half (4 ounces)
        8 flour tortillas
        1 cup chopped lettuce
        1 medium tomato, chopped

Combine beans, *2 tablespoons* of chili peppers, onion, and salt. Add beef; mix well. Form into eight 5-inch patties. Place ½ cheese slice on each; fold to seal cheese inside, forming semicircle. Grill over *medium* coals 5 to 6 minutes; turn and grill 4 to 5 minutes. Heat tortillas on grill. Serve burgers in hot tortillas. Add lettuce, tomato, and remaining chili peppers as desired. Serves 8.

Barbecued Beef Burgers

        1 beaten egg
        2 tablespoons milk
        2 tablespoons catsup
        ¼ cup finely crushed saltine
            crackers (4 crackers)
        1 pound ground beef
        4 thin slices onion
        4 slices sharp American cheese
        ¼ cup chopped onion
        ¼ cup butter *or* margarine
        ¼ cup catsup
        2 tablespoons packed brown sugar
        ½ teaspoon prepared horseradish

Combine egg, milk, 2 tablespoons catsup, crumbs, and ½ teaspoon salt; add beef and mix well. Shape into four patties; place each on a 12-inch square of heavy-duty foil. Top *each* with 1 slice onion and 1 slice cheese. Cook chopped onion in butter till tender but not brown. Add ¼ cup catsup, brown sugar, horseradish, and ½ teaspoon salt; simmer, uncovered, 5 minutes. Spoon over burgers. Wrap foil loosely around meat, sealing edges well. Cook over *medium* coals, onion side down, for 15 minutes. Turn; cook till meat is done, 10 minutes. Serves 4.

Stuffed Steak Sandwiches
Special treatment for budget-wise flank steaks—

        2 1-pound beef flank steaks
            Instant non-seasoned meat
            tenderizer
        2 tablespoons prepared
            horseradish
        ⅓ cup chopped onion
        ⅓ cup chopped celery
        2 tablespoons butter, melted
        ½ teaspoon seasoned salt
        1 cup dairy sour cream
        12 slices French bread, toasted
            and buttered

Score steaks on both sides. Use tenderizer according to label directions. Spread one side of steaks with horseradish. Combine onion, celery, butter, and seasoned salt; spread on steaks. Roll up jelly-roll style, fasten with skewers, and tie with string. Balance meat rolls on spit; secure with holding forks. Place *medium* coals on both sides of drip pan. Attach spit so meat is over drip pan; turn on motor. Roast over *medium* coals till done, about 45 minutes. Let stand a few minutes; remove strings and skewers. Heat sour cream over low heat; *do not boil.* Carefully cut meat rolls into thin slices and place on bread. Spoon warm sour cream over meat. Sprinkle with paprika, if desired. Makes 6 servings.

Mustard-Brushed Bologna Kabobs
Serve these as an appetizer if desired—

        1 pound chunk bologna, cut into
            1-inch cubes
        1 13¼-ounce can pineapple chunks,
            drained
        ¼ cup butter or margarine, melted
        2 tablespoons Dijon-style mustard
        1 tablespoon snipped parsley
        2 teaspoons lemon juice
            Dash pepper

On skewers alternately thread bologna cubes with pineapple chunks. Combine butter, mustard, parsley, lemon juice, and pepper. Brush over skewered bologna and pineapple. Cook kabobs over *medium* coals, turning frequently till heated through, 8 to 10 minutes. Brush frequently with the butter mixture. Serves 4.

Hot-Style Eye of Round

    1 3-pound beef eye of round roast
      Instant non-seasoned meat
        tenderizer
    1 cup hot-style catsup
    ½ cup water
    2 tablespoons Worcestershire
        sauce
    1 clove garlic, minced
    ½ teaspoon chili powder
    ¼ teaspoon salt

Sprinkle all sides of roast evenly with tenderizer, using ½ teaspoon per pound of meat. To ensure penetration, pierce all sides deeply at ½-inch intervals with long-tined fork. In saucepan combine remaining ingredients; simmer 5 minutes. Insert spit rod through center of roast. Adjust holding forks and test balance. Insert meat thermometer. Place *medium-hot* coals on both sides of drip pan. Attach spit so roast is over drip pan. Turn on motor; lower hood. Roast over *medium-hot* coals till meat thermometer registers 140° for rare (1½ hours), 160° for medium, and 170° for well-done. Baste last 30 minutes with sauce. Pass sauce. Serves 8.

Picnic Chicken Sandwiches

    1 4¾- or 5-ounce can chicken
        spread
    ¼ cup finely chopped celery
    2 tablespoons bacon-flavor
        protein bits
      Mayonnaise *or* salad dressing
    8 slices rye bread
      Butter *or* margarine

Stir together chicken spread, celery, and protein bits; add enough mayonnaise to moisten. Spread bread slices with butter. Spread 4 slices of the buttered rye bread with filling. Cover with remaining 4 slices of bread, buttered side down. Makes 4 servings.

◀ **Treat guests to an elegant cookout** by combining *Hot-Style Eye of Round* and *Skewered Stuffed Mushrooms* (see recipe, page 40). A generous seasoning of chili powder and hot-style catsup adds zip to the meat. Wrap stuffed mushroom caps in foil and heat over the coals.

Company Pork Loin Roast

    1 cup catsup
    ¼ cup cooking oil
    ¼ cup wine vinegar
    2 tablespoons instant minced
        onion
    2 tablespoons Worcestershire
        sauce
    1 tablespoon packed brown sugar
    1 teaspoon mustard seed
    1 teaspoon dried oregano, crushed
    1 bay leaf
    ½ teaspoon cracked pepper
    ¼ teaspoon chili powder
    1 5-pound boneless pork loin
        roast, rolled and tied

In saucepan combine catsup, cooking oil, wine vinegar, onion, Worcestershire sauce, brown sugar, mustard seed, oregano, bay leaf, pepper, chili powder, ½ cup water, and ½ teaspoon salt. Simmer 20 minutes; remove bay leaf.

Insert spit rod through center of roast. Adjust holding forks and test balance. Insert meat thermometer. Place *medium-hot* coals on both sides of drip pan. Attach spit so roast is over drip pan. Turn on motor; lower hood. Roast till meat thermometer registers 170°, for 2 to 2½ hours. Brush with sauce frequently during last 30 to 45 minutes. Serves 8.

Glazed Pork Kabobs

    ½ cup apricot preserves
    ½ of an 8-ounce can tomato sauce
    ¼ cup packed brown sugar
    ¼ cup dry red wine
    2 tablespoons lemon juice
    2 tablespoons cooking oil
    1 teaspoon onion juice
    1½ pounds lean boneless pork,
        cut in 1-inch pieces
    4 large carrots, cut in 1-inch
        pieces and cooked
      Fresh pineapple chunks

Combine first 7 ingredients. Cook, uncovered, 10 to 15 minutes; stir occasionally. Thread pork, carrots, and pineapple on 6 skewers; season with salt and pepper. Grill over *medium* coals 10 minutes; turn frequently. Brush with sauce; grill 5 minutes more. Serves 6.

German-Style Barbecued Franks

8 frankfurters
1 8-ounce can sauerkraut, drained
2 teaspoons prepared mustard
8 slices bacon, partially cooked
    and drained
8 frankfurter buns
    Thousand Island salad dressing

Split franks lengthwise almost to opposite side. Combine sauerkraut and mustard; spoon into the franks. Wrap a bacon strip around each and secure with wooden picks. Grill over *medium* coals for 5 minutes, turning frequently. Split and toast buns; spread with salad dressing. Place bacon-wrapped frank in each. Serves 8.

Grilled Bratwursts

1 pound bratwurst (6 brats)
¼ cup light cream
2 tablespoons prepared mustard
½ teaspoon instant minced onion
¼ teaspoon coarse cracked pepper
    Dash paprika
1 16-ounce can sauerkraut,
    drained

Cut each brat in thirds. Thread on four skewers. Blend cream, mustard, onion, pepper, and paprika. Grill brat pieces over *medium-hot* coals for 7 to 8 minutes, brushing often with sauce. In a saucepan heat sauerkraut. Serve grilled meat and sauce over hot sauerkraut. Serves 4.

Smoky Chicken Roasts

2 2- to 2½-pound ready-to-cook
    broiler-fryer chickens
½ cup cooking oil
¼ cup lemon juice

Salt chicken cavities; truss. Insert spit rod through centers of birds. Adjust holding forks; test balance. Soak hickory chips in water. Place *medium* coals on both sides of drip pan. Combine oil and lemon juice; brush on birds. Attach spit so birds are over drip pan. Turn on motor. Roast over *medium* coals for 1½ hours, brushing frequently with lemon mixture and sprinkling coals with hickory chips every 15 minutes. Makes 6 servings.

Lemonade Chicken

1 6-ounce can frozen lemonade
    concentrate, thawed
⅓ cup soy sauce
1 teaspoon seasoned salt
½ teaspoon celery salt
⅛ teaspoon garlic powder
2 2½- to 3-pound ready-to-cook
    broiler-fryer chickens, cut up

In screw-top jar combine thawed lemonade concentrate, soy sauce, seasoned salt, celery salt, and garlic powder. Cover; shake vigorously to blend. Pour into small bowl. Dip chicken pieces in lemonade mixture. Grill chicken over *medium-hot* coals for 45 to 50 minutes, brushing with lemonade mixture and turning frequently. Garnish with lemon twists and parsley, if desired. Makes 8 servings.

Plum-Glazed Turkey Roasts
Perfect for an outdoor buffet; shown on page 41 —

2 28-ounce rolled turkey roasts,
    thawed
1 30-ounce can purple plums
¼ cup frozen orange juice
    concentrate, thawed
2 tablespoons sugar
½ teaspoon Worcestershire
    sauce

Tie each turkey roast together securely with twine, if necessary. Insert spit rod through center of roasts and attach holding forks; test balance. Wrap turkey roasts tightly in foil, crimping ends of foil against spit rod close to roasts. Attach spit; turn on motor. Roast over *medium-hot* coals for 2 hours.

Meanwhile, prepare plum sauce. Drain plums, reserving ½ cup syrup. Press plums through a sieve. In saucepan combine plum purée, reserved syrup, orange juice concentrate, sugar, and Worcestershire sauce. Heat to boiling. Simmer, uncovered till mixture reaches desired consistency, 15 to 20 minutes. After the roasts have cooked for 2 hours, remove foil and brush roasts with plum sauce. Insert roast meat thermometer. Continue roasting till thermometer registers 175°, about 15 minutes longer. Let roasts stand 10 minutes before slicing. Spoon remaining sauce over turkey. Serves 10 to 12.

Ham-Yam Kabobs

A grilled version of traditional holiday fare—

> 1 teaspoon cornstarch
> 1 6-ounce can frozen pineapple
>   juice concentrate, thawed
> ½ cup chili sauce
> 3 tablespoons honey
> 2 tablespoons cooking oil
> 1 teaspoon prepared horseradish
> 2¼ pounds fresh yams, cooked,
>   peeled, and cut in
>   1½-inch pieces
> 2 pounds fully cooked ham,
>   cut in 1½-inch pieces
> 1 medium green pepper, cubed

In small saucepan combine cornstarch with *2 tablespoons* of the pineapple concentrate. Stir in remaining concentrate, chili sauce, honey, oil, and horseradish. Cook, stirring constantly, till sauce comes to boiling. Boil 1 minute.

Thread yams, ham, and green pepper alternately on 6 skewers. Grill over *medium* coals for 15 to 20 minutes, brushing frequently with sauce. Pass remaining sauce. Makes 6 servings.

Apricot-Stuffed Pork Chops

Grilled and topped with an apricot sauce—

> 6 pork rib chops, cut
>   1 inch thick
> 1 17-ounce can apricot halves
> ¼ cup catsup
> 2 tablespoons chopped onion
> 2 tablespoons cooking oil
> 1 tablespoon lemon juice
> ½ teaspoon dry mustard

Cut pocket in each chop by cutting from fat side almost to bone edge. Season cavity with a little salt and pepper. Drain apricots, reserving ½ cup syrup. Place two apricot halves in pocket of each chop. Cut up remaining apricots; set aside. Grill chops over *medium* coals for 40 minutes, turning once. During the last 5 minutes, brush chops frequently with sauce.

To prepare sauce, in saucepan combine the reserved apricot juice and cut-up apricots with the catsup, onion, oil, lemon juice, and dry mustard. Heat to boiling; reduce heat and simmer for 15 minutes. Serve the remaining sauce with the grilled chops. Serves 6.

Golden Glazed Ribs

> 4 pounds pork loin back ribs,
>   cut in serving-size pieces
> 1½ cups water
> 1 cup snipped dried apricots
> ½ cup packed brown sugar
> 2 tablespoons vinegar
> 1 tablespoon lemon juice
> 1 teaspoon ground ginger
> ½ teaspoon salt

Place ribs in large saucepan or Dutch oven; cover with salted water. Cover and simmer till ribs are tender, about 1 hour. Drain well and season ribs with a little salt and pepper.

While ribs are cooking, prepare the glaze by combining water, apricots, brown sugar, vinegar, lemon juice, ginger, and salt. Bring to boiling. Reduce heat; cover and simmer 5 minutes. Pour mixture into blender container; cover and blend till smooth. Brush over ribs.

Place ribs on grill over *medium-slow* coals for 20 to 30 minutes. Turn once or twice and brush occasionally with glaze. Serves 4.

Teriyaki Smoked Pork Loin

Serve with pineapple for a South Seas luau party—

> 1 4- to 5-pound boneless rolled
>   pork loin roast
>   • • •
> ⅔ cup soy sauce
> ¼ cup cooking oil
> 2 tablespoons molasses
> 2 teaspoons dry mustard
> 2 teaspoons ground ginger
> 2 cloves garlic, minced

Insert spit rod through center of roast. Adjust holding forks; test balance. Insert meat thermometer near center of roast but not touching metal rod. Soak hickory chips in water. Place *medium* coals on both sides of drip pan. Attach spit so roast is over drip pan; turn on motor. Add damp hickory chips to coals; lower smoke hood. Roast till meat thermometer registers 170°, about 3 hours. After first hour, brush roast with a sauce made by combining the soy sauce, cooking oil, molasses, dry mustard, ginger, and minced garlic. Let the cooked roast stand about 15 minutes before carving. Makes 12 to 15 servings.

Hot-Style Beans and Tomatoes

Mustard and horseradish spark this combination —

**8 ounces fresh green beans,
cut in 1-inch pieces
2 tomatoes, sliced
¼ cup chopped onion
¼ cup butter *or* margarine,
softened
1 tablespoon packed brown sugar
2 teaspoons prepared mustard
1 teaspoon salt
1 teaspoon prepared horseradish**

Cook green beans in a little boiling water for 10 minutes. Drain and place on a large double-thickness sheet of heavy foil. Top with the tomato slices. Combine chopped onion, butter, brown sugar, mustard, salt, horseradish, and dash pepper; beat till fluffy.

Dot seasoned butter over beans and tomatoes. Wrap vegetables tightly in foil, sealing edges. Cook over *medium-hot* coals till done, 30 to 35 minutes. Makes 4 or 5 servings.

Skewered Stuffed Mushrooms

"Sandwich" the caps as shown on page 36 —

**20 large fresh mushrooms
(about 10 ounces)
⅓ cup dry white wine
1 teaspoon instant chicken
bouillon granules
¼ cup finely chopped onion
2 tablespoons butter *or* margarine
½ cup herb-seasoned stuffing mix,
crushed
Butter *or* margarine, melted**

Separate mushroom caps and stems. In saucepan heat wine and bouillon till granules dissolve. Add mushroom caps to liquid in saucepan; cover and simmer 2 minutes. Drain on paper toweling. Reserve ¼ cup liquid. Finely chop mushroom stems to make ½ cup; cook with onion in 2 tablespoons butter till tender. Stir in stuffing mix and ¼ cup reserved wine liquid. Fit 2 mushroom caps together with 1 tablespoon stuffing between. Thread on skewers. Brush with melted butter; wrap in heavy foil. Place over *medium-hot* coals for 3 to 5 minutes. Remove foil. Add tomato wedges and green pepper pieces to skewers, if desired. Makes 10.

Mushroom-Rice Bake

Cooks in a foil pouch directly on the grill —

**1⅓ cups quick-cooking rice
1 cup cold water
1 3-ounce can sliced mushrooms
¼ cup finely chopped onion
1 teaspoon Worcestershire sauce
½ teaspoon salt
2 tablespoons butter *or* margarine**

Tear off a 36-inch length of 18-inch-wide heavy foil. Fold in half to make a square. Fold up sides, using fist to form a pouch. Thoroughly combine rice, water, undrained mushrooms, onion, Worcestershire sauce, and salt. Place in pouch; dot with butter. Fold edges of foil to seal pouch tightly. Place on grill over *hot* coals and heat 15 to 18 minutes. Before serving, fluff rice with a fork. Makes 4 servings.

Classy Carrots

In saucepan prepare one 16-ounce package frozen crinkle-cut carrots according to package directions; drain. Stir in ¼ cup orange marmalade, 2 tablespoons butter, and 1 tablespoon orange liqueur. Simmer, stirring gently over low heat, till butter is melted and carrots are coated with the sauce. Season to taste with salt and pepper. Makes 4 or 5 servings.

Barbecued Beans and Bacon

**2 16-ounce cans pork and
beans in tomato sauce
¾ cup packed brown sugar
1 teaspoon dry mustard
6 slices bacon, cut in small
pieces
½ cup catsup**

Empty *one* of the cans of beans into 1½-quart heavy metal casserole. Combine brown sugar and mustard; sprinkle *half* of mixture over beans. Top with second can of beans; sprinkle with remaining brown sugar mixture. Top with bacon. Spread catsup over all. Arrange 3 or 4 additional slices of bacon on top, if desired. Cook, covered, over *slow* coals about 1 hour. (If hood of grill is down, do not cover beans.) Makes 6 to 8 servings.

Plum-Glazed Turkey Roasts (see recipe, page 38) with a hot Vegetable Skillet are company fare for outdoor dining. Fix two roasts for a crowd.

Crushed savory flavors the garden vegetable combination. Cook the vegetables indoors, then whisk them out to the patio when guests arrive.

Vegetable Skillet

    2 medium onions, thinly sliced
        (1 cup)
    2 tablespoons butter
        or margarine
    4 medium zucchini, thinly sliced
        (5 cups)
    1 3-ounce can sliced mushrooms
    1 teaspoon salt
    ½ teaspoon dried savory, crushed
        Dash pepper
    2 tomatoes, cut in wedges

In 10-inch skillet cook onion in butter till crisp-tender. Add zucchini. Drain mushrooms, reserving 2 tablespoons of the liquid. To skillet add mushrooms with reserved liquid, salt, savory, and pepper. Mix well. Cover and cook till zucchini is crisp-tender, about 5 minutes. Add tomatoes and heat through, about 1 minute longer. Makes 6 servings.

Vegetables on a Stick
Scallop-edge pattypan squash make these unusual —

    6 small onions
    5 small pattypan squash
    2 sweet red peppers
            • • •
    ¼ cup butter or margarine
    ¼ teaspoon salt
        Dash pepper

Partially cook onions in small amount of boiling salted water till nearly tender, about 25 minutes; drain. Cut the pattypan squash into quarters. Cut the red peppers into large squares. In small saucepan combine butter, salt, and pepper; heat till butter melts. On four skewers alternately thread wedges of squash, the onions, and pepper squares.

Grill over *medium* coals till done, 20 to 25 minutes. Turn frequently and brush with the seasoned melted butter. Makes 4 servings.

Onion Potatoes

6 medium baking potatoes
½ cup butter *or* margarine,
    softened
1 envelope onion soup mix

Scrub potatoes and cut each crosswise into ½-inch-thick slices. Blend butter with the soup mix. Spread on one side of each potato slice. Reassemble potatoes; wrap each in heavy foil, sealing well. Bake on grill over *medium* coals till done, 45 to 60 minutes. Turn often. Serve with sour cream, if desired. Serves 6.

Cheesy Potato-Bacon Bake

3 large baking potatoes, peeled
4 or 5 slices bacon, crisp-cooked,
    drained, and crumbled
1 large onion, sliced
2 cups cubed sharp American
    cheese (8 ounces)
½ cup butter *or* margarine

Slice potatoes onto a large sheet of heavy foil. Sprinkle with a little salt, pepper, and the bacon. Add onion and cheese cubes. Dot butter over all. Mix on the foil.

Bring edges of foil up, leaving space for expansion of steam. Seal well with a double fold. Place package on grill and cook over *slow* coals till done, about 1 hour. Turn several times. Makes 4 to 6 servings.

Cheese-Topped Tomatoes

2 tomatoes
¾ cup soft bread crumbs
    (1 slice bread)
½ cup shredded sharp American
    cheese (2 ounces)
2 tablespoons butter *or*
    margarine, melted
2 tablespoons snipped parsley

Slice tomatoes in half with a sawtooth cut. Season with a little salt and pepper. Combine bread crumbs, cheese, and butter; sprinkle over tomatoes. Garnish with parsley. Wrap tomatoes loosely in foil. Heat over *medium-hot* coals till warmed through, 15 to 20 minutes. Serve immediately. Makes 4 servings.

Chili-Style Potato Salad
South-of-the-border version of an old favorite—

4 medium potatoes
⅓ cup salad oil
¼ cup vinegar
1 tablespoon sugar
1½ teaspoons chili powder
1 teaspoon seasoned salt
    Dash bottled hot pepper
    sauce
        • • •
1 8-ounce can whole kernel corn,
    drained
1 small onion, thinly sliced
    and separated into rings
½ cup shredded carrot
½ cup chopped green pepper
½ cup sliced pitted ripe olives

Cook potatoes in boiling salted water till tender, 35 to 40 minutes. Drain, peel, and cut into cubes. Combine oil, vinegar, sugar, chili powder, seasoned salt, and hot pepper sauce. Add to warm potatoes; toss gently to coat. Cover and chill 1 hour.

Combine corn, onion, carrot, green pepper, and olives. Fold into chilled potatoes. Garnish with additional halved ripe olives, if desired. Serve chilled. Makes 6 to 8 servings.

Tomatoes Rosé
An Italian-seasoned marinade gives flavor tang—

4 large tomatoes
½ cup rosé wine
⅓ cup salad oil
¼ cup finely chopped celery
¼ cup finely sliced green onion
3 tablespoons wine vinegar
1 envelope Italian salad
    dressing mix
    Lettuce leaves
    Celery leaves

Wash, peel, and thinly slice tomatoes; place in shallow dish or deep bowl. Combine wine, oil, celery, green onion, vinegar, and salad dressing mix. Pour over tomatoes. Cover and chill several hours. Lift tomatoes from marinade and place on lettuce leaves. Spoon some of the dressing over the top and pass the remaining. Garnish with celery leaves. Makes 6 servings.

Wilted Escarole-Bacon Salad

6 slices bacon
¼ cup vinegar
1½ teaspoons sugar
⅛ teaspoon salt
¼ cup sliced green onion
6 cups torn escarole *or*
   leaf lettuce
1 tablespoon toasted sesame seed

In large skillet cook bacon till crisp; drain, reserving 2 tablespoons drippings. Crumble bacon; set aside. Stir vinegar, sugar, salt, and dash of pepper into reserved drippings; bring to boiling. Add green onion. Gradually add escarole or lettuce to skillet, tossing just till the greens are coated and slightly wilted. Remove from heat. Add crumbled bacon and sesame seed; toss lightly. Makes 6 servings.

Taco Cabbage Salad

Try the stronger-flavored savoy cabbage in this—

4 cups chopped cabbage
1 15-ounce can red kidney beans,
   drained
2 medium tomatoes, chopped
⅓ cup sliced pimiento-stuffed
   green olives
1 large avocado, pitted, peeled,
   and mashed (⅔ cup)
½ cup dairy sour cream
⅓ cup milk
1 tablespoon finely chopped onion
1 tablespoon Italian salad
   dressing
1 tablespoon lemon juice
½ teaspoon Worcestershire sauce
¼ teaspoon salt
½ cup shredded sharp Cheddar
   cheese (2 ounces)
½ cup coarsely crushed corn chips

Chill all ingredients except corn chips. In a large chilled bowl place chopped cabbage, drained beans, chopped tomatoes, and sliced olives.

Make the dressing by combining the mashed avocado, sour cream, milk, chopped onion, salad dressing, lemon juice, Worcestershire sauce, and salt. Pour dressing over vegetables in bowl and toss lightly. Sprinkle cheese and corn chips over the top. Serve immediately. Serves 6.

Bean-Macaroni Salad

2 cups cooked macaroni
1 16-ounce can three-bean
   salad
1 cup chopped celery
3 hard-cooked eggs, coarsely
   chopped
½ cup creamy French salad
   dressing
¼ cup sweet pickle relish
½ teaspoon salt
   Several drops bottled hot
   pepper sauce
   Dash pepper

In a large bowl combine cooked macaroni, *undrained* three-bean salad, celery, and coarsely chopped eggs. Blend together French dressing, pickle relish, salt, hot pepper sauce, and pepper. Pour over macaroni mixture; toss lightly. Chill at least 1 hour. Garnish with additional hard-cooked eggs, if desired. Makes 8 to 10 servings.

Blueberry-Melon Salad

Show off plump, fresh blueberries in melon "bowls"—

⅓ cup blueberry preserves
1 3-ounce package cream cheese,
   softened
1 tablespoon milk
½ teaspoon grated lemon peel
2 teaspoons lemon juice
½ cup whipping cream
2 small honeydew melons
   Leaf lettuce
1½ cups cream-style cottage cheese
1 cup fresh blueberries

Gradually blend preserves into cream cheese. Stir in the milk, lemon peel, and lemon juice. Whip the cream just till soft peaks form; fold into cream cheese mixture. Chill.

Cut melons in half and remove seeds. Use a melon baller to scoop out pulp. Line melon shells with leaf lettuce. Divide melon balls among lined shells. Mound a generous ⅓ cup cottage cheese in center of each. Place ¼ cup blueberries around each mound.

Drizzle some of the chilled blueberry preserve and cream cheese dressing over each. Makes 4 servings.

Caesar's Chicken Salad is a hearty variation of the first Caesar salad created by an Italian restaurateur in Tijuana, Mexico, and popularized by American tourists. Strips of cooked chicken are tossed with romaine and artichoke hearts, then topped with seasoned oil dressing.

Caesar's Chicken Salad

>   1 tablespoon butter
>   *or* margarine
>   ½ cup plain croutons
>   ⅛ teaspoon garlic salt
>   4 cups torn romaine
>   2 cups cooked chicken* cut
>   in julienne strips
>   (12 ounces)
>   1 7-ounce can artichoke hearts,
>   drained and halved
>   2 tablespoons grated
>   Parmesan cheese
>   Caesar Salad Dressing

In small skillet melt butter; add the croutons. Cook and stir till lightly browned. Remove from heat; sprinkle with garlic salt. Set aside. Rub a large salad bowl with a cut clove of garlic, if desired. Add the romaine, cooked chicken strips, halved artichoke hearts, Parmesan cheese, and croutons. Pour the Caesar Salad Dressing over and toss salad, mixing thoroughly. Makes 6 servings.

Caesar Salad Dressing

>   3 anchovy fillets
>   ¼ cup salad oil *or* olive oil
>   ½ teaspoon dry mustard
>   Dash freshly ground pepper
>   2 tablespoons lemon juice
>   1 teaspoon Worcestershire sauce
>   1 egg

In bowl cream together anchovies, *1 tablespoon* oil, dry mustard, and pepper. Blend in lemon juice, Worcestershire sauce, and remaining oil; set aside. Break egg into about 1 cup boiling water. Immediately remove from heat; let stand 1 minute. Remove egg from water. Cool slightly; add to anchovy mixture. Beat till dressing becomes creamy. Makes about ⅔ cup.

Note: To prepare chicken, place one 1-pound whole chicken breast in saucepan with water to cover. Simmer till meat is tender, 20 to 25 minutes; chill. Remove bones and skin. Cut chicken meat into strips. Makes 2 cups.

Lemon-Peppered Buns

> ½ cup butter *or* margarine,
>   softened
> ¼ cup snipped parsley
> 2 teaspoons soy sauce
> 1 teaspoon lemon pepper marinade
> 8 frankfurter buns

Combine butter, parsley, soy sauce, and lemon pepper marinade. Split buns; spread cut surfaces with butter mixture. Grill over *slow* coals for 8 to 10 minutes. Makes 8 servings.

Onion Buns

A hot roll mix makes these quick to fix —

> 1¼ cups finely chopped onion
> 2 tablespoons butter *or* margarine
> 1 13¾-ounce package hot roll mix
> 1 egg
> 1 tablespoon milk
> ⅛ teaspoon salt

Cook onion in butter till tender but not brown; set aside. Prepare roll dough according to package directions, adding *2 tablespoons* of the cooked onion. Cover; let rise in warm place till double (45 to 60 minutes). Slightly beat the egg. Stir *1 tablespoon* egg into remaining cooked onion; stir in milk and salt.

   With lightly floured hands, shape the dough into 12 round buns. Place on a greased baking sheet. Using fingers, make a large indentation in the center of each bun. Spoon about *2 teaspoons* of the onion mixture into each indentation. Brush tops with reserved egg. Sprinkle with poppy seed, if desired. Cover; let rise till double (45 to 60 minutes). Bake at 375° for 20 to 25 minutes. Makes 12 rolls.

Grilled Blueberry Muffin Bread

Lightly grease two 9-inch foil pie pans. Prepare 1 13½-ounce package blueberry muffin mix according to package directions; pour into one pan. Cover with second pan, inverted. Fasten rims together with spring-type clothespins. Place on grill over *slow* coals for 15 minutes per side, rotating pan occasionally for even baking. Remove top pan; cut bread into wedges. Serve with butter. Makes 6 servings.

Zippy French Loaves

Seasoned mini-loaves to serve with grilled meat —

> 1 3-ounce package cream cheese
>   with chives, softened
> 2 tablespoons butter *or* margarine,
>   softened
> 1 teaspoon Italian seasoning
> ¼ teaspoon cracked black pepper
> ⅛ teaspoon garlic salt
> 8 French rolls

Combine cream cheese, softened butter, Italian seasoning, pepper, and garlic salt. Split the French rolls lengthwise, *cutting to but not through* opposite side of roll. Spread cream cheese mixture inside rolls. Wrap loosely in foil. Heat over *medium-hot* coals for 8 to 10 minutes. Makes 8 servings.

Sauerkraut-Rye Bread

Excellent with corned beef and Swiss cheese —

> 1 package active dry yeast
> 2 cups rye flour
> ¾ cup water
> 2 tablespoons butter *or* margarine
> 2 teaspoons sugar
> 1 teaspoon salt
> 1 egg
> 1 8-ounce can sauerkraut, rinsed,
>   well-drained, and snipped
> 1¼ to 1½ cups all-purpose flour
> 1 beaten egg

In large mixing bowl combine yeast and *1 cup* of the rye flour. In saucepan heat the water, butter, sugar, and salt just till warm (115-120°), stirring to melt the butter. Add to dry mixture in mixing bowl; add 1 egg.

   Beat at low speed of electric mixer for ½ minute, scraping sides of bowl constantly. Beat 3 minutes at high speed. By hand, stir in drained and snipped sauerkraut, the remaining 1 cup rye flour, and enough of the all-purpose flour to make a moderately stiff dough. Knead till smooth and elastic, 8 to 10 minutes. Place in a greased bowl; turn once. Cover and let rise till double (50 to 60 minutes). Punch down; place in greased 1½ quart casserole. Cover and let rise 45 to 60 minutes. Brush top of loaf with the beaten egg. Bake at 400° for 30 to 35 minutes. Makes 1 loaf.

Hawaiian Blueberry Pie

Pineapple topping adds the tropical flavor—

Pastry for 9-inch
    lattice-top pie
1 12-ounce jar pineapple topping
3 tablespoons all-purpose flour
½ teaspoon grated lemon peel
4 cups fresh *or* frozen
    blueberries, thawed
1 tablespoon butter *or* margarine

Line a 9-inch pie plate with pastry. In large bowl combine pineapple topping, flour, and grated lemon peel. Fold in blueberries. Pour into pastry shell. Dot with butter. Adjust the lattice top; seal and flute edges. Bake at 400° for 35 to 40 minutes.

Rhubarb-Cherry Pie

Pastry for 9-inch
    lattice-top pie
2 cups sliced rhubarb
1 21-ounce can cherry pie filling
¾ cup sugar
2½ tablespoons quick-cooking
    tapioca

Line a 9-inch pie plate with pastry. In bowl combine rhubarb, pie filling, sugar, and tapioca. Let stand 15 minutes. Spoon into pastry shell. Adjust lattice top; seal and flute edges. Bake at 400° for 40 to 45 minutes.

Grilled Pineapple Rings

1 small or medium pineapple,
    peeled
½ cup maple-flavored syrup
½ teaspoon ground cinnamon
3 spiced whole crab apples
30 whole cloves (optional)

Cut pineapple crosswise into 6 slices about ¾ inch thick. Cut out cores, leaving center holes about 1½ inches in diameter. Blend syrup and cinnamon. Halve crab apples. Fit one half in center of each ring; secure with metal skewer. If desired, insert whole cloves in outside of each ring. Grill over *medium-slow* coals about 3 minutes per side; brush frequently with syrup mixture. Makes 6 servings.

Sunflower Seed Cookies

½ cup butter *or* margarine
½ cup packed brown sugar
½ cup granulated sugar
1 egg
½ teaspoon vanilla
1½ cups quick-cooking rolled oats
¾ cup whole wheat flour
½ teaspoon baking soda
¼ teaspoon salt
¾ cup shelled sunflower seed

Cream together butter and sugars. Add egg and vanilla; beat well. Combine oats, flour, soda, and salt. Stir into creamed mixture. Stir in sunflower seed. Shape dough into 2 rolls, each about 1½ inches in diameter. Wrap in waxed paper or clear plastic wrap; chill thoroughly. Slice ¼ inch thick and place 2 inches apart on ungreased cookie sheet. Bake at 350° for 10 minutes. Cool on wire racks. Makes 54.

Fresh Fruit Melon Compote

1 cup white grape juice
½ cup orange marmalade
¼ cup orange liqueur
1 watermelon*
1 pint whole strawberries,
    hulled
2 cups seedless green grapes
2 cups honeydew melon balls
2 cups cantaloupe balls
1 cup blueberries

Blend grape juice, marmalade, and liqueur. Set aside. Remove top one-fourth of watermelon, cutting a scalloped edge. If necessary, cut a thin slice from bottom of watermelon so it will sit level. Scoop out melon pulp with melon ball cutter, making melon balls. Combine *2 cups* of the watermelon balls (use remaining as desired), with strawberries, grapes, honeydew melon balls, cantaloupe balls, and blueberries. Pour grape juice mixture over; stir gently. Chill 1 to 2 hours, stirring once or twice. Place fruit and juices in melon shell. Serves 10 to 12.
*Note: If desired, draw a design on watermelon shell with a soft lead pencil. Carve, using an art knife with a ¹⁄₁₆- to ⅛-inch blade. Be careful to remove only the green skin; do not pierce through to the white rind.

Spiced Beer Cake

        1 cup light molasses
    ⅓ cup cooking oil
        2 eggs
    2½ cups all-purpose flour
    1½ teaspoons baking soda
    ½ teaspoon ground ginger
    ¼ teaspoon ground cinnamon
    ¼ teaspoon ground cloves
    ¼ teaspoon ground nutmeg
    ½ cup dark *or* light beer
        1 cup raisins
    ½ cup chopped walnuts
        Buttered Beer Sauce

In mixing bowl combine molasses and oil. Beat in eggs. Stir together flour, soda, ginger, cinnamon, cloves, and nutmeg. Beat into molasses mixture alternately with beer. Stir in raisins and nuts. Pour into greased and floured 13x9x2-inch baking pan. Bake at 350° for 25 to 30 minutes. Remove from oven; cool slightly and cut in squares to serve. Top with Buttered Beer Sauce and serve warm. Serves 12 to 15.

Buttered Beer Sauce: In saucepan combine ¼ cup packed brown sugar and 4 teaspoons all-purpose flour. Gradually stir in ½ cup beer and ½ cup water. Cook and stir till thickened and bubbly. Stir in 2 tablespoons butter and ¼ teaspoon vanilla; heat through. Makes 1¼ cups.

Chocolate-Honey Ice Cream

    ½ cup semisweet chocolate pieces
        2 tablespoons all-purpose flour
    1½ cups milk
    ½ cup honey
        2 eggs
        2 cups whipping cream
    ½ teaspoon vanilla

In saucepan combine chocolate pieces, flour, and dash salt. Blend milk with honey. Gradually stir into chocolate mixture. Cook and stir over medium heat till chocolate melts and mixture thickens and bubbles. In bowl beat the eggs. Add a moderate amount of hot chocolate mixture to eggs; mix well. Return slowly to hot mixture. Cook and stir 1 minute more. Chill. Stir in cream and vanilla. Freeze in 2-quart ice cream freezer. Let ripen. Garnish with semisweet chocolate pieces, if desired. Makes 1½ quarts.

Camper's Hot Cocoa

Prepare dry mix at home and carry in a plastic bag—

        1 cup sugar
    ¾ cup unsweetened cocoa powder
        3 cups nonfat dry milk powder
        Dash salt
        8 cups water

In bowl combine sugar and cocoa powder; stir in milk powder and salt. Keep in covered container or plastic bag until needed. To serve, pour mix into saucepan; stir in *1 cup* of the water till blended. Stir in remaining water and heat through, but *do not boil.* Serves 8.

For 1 serving: Place ⅓ cup dry mixture in a cup. Stir in about 2 tablespoons cold water; mix well. Stir in boiling water to fill cup.

P-Nutty Cocoa

Everybody's favorite and so easy to make—

    ½ cup chocolate-flavored syrup
    ¼ cup peanut butter
        4 cups milk
        Marshmallows

In saucepan combine chocolate syrup and peanut butter. Add the milk, a little at a time, stirring till well blended. Heat almost to boiling, stirring occasionally. Pour into mugs or cups and top with marshmallows. Makes 6 servings.

Double Orange Sangria

Garnish each serving with an orange slice—

        1 orange
    ¼ cup sugar
        1 ⅘-quart bottle dry red wine
            (about 3¼ cups)
    ½ cup orange liqueur
        2 7-ounce bottles carbonated water,
            chilled (about 2 cups)

Thinly slice the outer peel from half the orange (use rest of orange as desired). Place peel and sugar in large pitcher. Press peel firmly against the pitcher with the back of a spoon. Stir in wine and liqueur. Chill. Just before serving, remove peel and pour in carbonated water, stirring lightly. Serve in tall glasses with ice and a slice of orange, if desired. Makes about 6 cups.

Meals that Families Cook Together

Let the whole family join in helping fix supper. Cooking together is great fun — especially when the menu includes Pot Roast Dip Sandwiches, Tomato-Bean Combo, Homemade Vanilla Ice Cream, and Oatmeal Chippers. (See index for recipe pages.)

Fun-for-All Menus

PIZZA SUPPER

Peppy Frank Pizzas
Totem Pole Relishes
Peanut Butter and Jelly Cake
Beer   Milk

Special Helps: If your family loves pizza, then this fun-to-fix meal is one that everyone will enjoy eating. Dad engineers the pizzas from the crust up. Use this quick-and-easy pizza topping, or be imaginative and create your own favorite topping. And, while you're putting the finishing touches on the cake, the children can thread skewers with pickles, olives, and vegetables for a salad.

Peppy Frank Pizzas

    1 13¾-ounce package hot roll mix
    2 tablespoons cooking oil
    1 15-ounce can pizza sauce
    1 pound frankfurters, thinly
        sliced
    ½ cup chopped green pepper
      Dried oregano, crushed
    1½ cups shredded American cheese

Soften yeast from roll mix in 1 cup warm water (110-115°); add dry ingredients from mix and blend well. Divide dough in half. On a lightly floured surface roll each half of the dough to a 13-inch circle. Transfer to a greased 12-inch pizza pan. Build up edges slightly.

Brush each pizza with *1 tablespoon* of the oil; spread each with *half* of the sauce. Sprinkle each with *half* of the franks and green pepper; sprinkle with oregano and top each with *half* of the cheese. Bake at 400° for 23 to 25 minutes. Garnish the pizzas with green pepper rings, if desired. Makes 2 pizzas.

Totem Pole Relishes

    1 small cucumber, cut in
        ½-inch slices
    8 pitted ripe olives
    8 cherry tomatoes
    1 10-ounce can jalapeño
        chili peppers, drained
    4 small sweet pickles
      Large onion

Thread first 5 ingredients on 4 skewers, placing pickles on the end. Stick skewers into the onion. Place on serving plate and garnish with endive, if desired. Makes 4 servings.

Peanut Butter and Jelly Cake

    2 cups all-purpose flour
    1½ cups sugar
    1 tablespoon baking powder
    1 cup milk
    ½ cup peanut butter
    ¼ cup shortening
    2 eggs
    1 10-ounce jar currant jelly
    1 package fluffy white frosting
        mix (for 2-layer cake)
    ½ cup chopped peanuts

In mixing bowl stir together flour, sugar, baking powder, and 1 teaspoon salt. Add milk, peanut butter, and shortening; beat 2 minutes at medium speed of electric mixer. Add eggs and beat mixture 2 minutes more. Pour into greased and lightly floured 13x9x2-inch baking pan. Bake at 350° till cake tests done, about 30 minutes. Cool. Break up currant jelly with fork; spread evenly over cake. Prepare frosting mix, following package directions. Carefully spread frosting over jelly on cake; sprinkle with nuts. Cut in squares. Makes 1 cake.

Homemade pizza is always a big hit with families, and you'll find *Peppy Frank Pizzas* no exception. Accompany this menu with *Totem Pole Relishes* and *Peanut Butter and Jelly Cake*.

FAMILY SUPPER
(See photo, page 48)

Pot Roast Dip Sandwiches
Individual Italian Rolls
(see recipe, page 62)
Tomato-Bean Combo
Homemade Vanilla Ice Cream
Oatmeal Chippers
(see recipe, page 63)
Coffee   Milk

Special Helps: The day before your supper, prepare both the rolls and the cookies. Let the children be the cooks in charge of making the cookies while you bake the yeast rolls. Help them learn the various cookiemaking techniques and supervise the oven baking.

The next afternoon, put the roast in the oven and prepare the salad so it can chill. The man in your family can get into the act, too, by making the ice cream. Remember to plan so the ice cream can ripen before serving time.

Homemade Vanilla Ice Cream

    4 cups milk
    2 cups sugar
½ teaspoon salt
    4 beaten eggs
    2 13-ounce cans evaporated milk
    2 cups light cream
    4 teaspoons vanilla
    Ice cream toppings

In large saucepan combine the 4 cups milk, sugar, and salt. Cook and stir until hot (do not boil). Gradually add a moderate amount of hot mixture to the eggs, mixing thoroughly; return to hot mixture. Cook and stir for 2 minutes. Cool to room temperature. Stir in the evaporated milk, light cream, and vanilla. Freeze in ice cream freezer according to manufacturer's directions. Serve with toppings. Makes 3½ quarts ice cream.

Pot Roast Dip Sandwiches
Use the remaining roast for hash or One-Crust Frozen Pot Pies (see recipe, page 92)—

    1 3-pound beef rump roast
¼ cup all-purpose flour
    2 tablespoons shortening
    Salt
    Pepper
½ cup water
    1 10½-ounce can condensed
       beef broth
    1 teaspoon instant minced onion
½ teaspoon Worcestershire sauce
    Individual Italian Rolls
    (see recipe, page 62)

Coat roast with flour. In Dutch oven or large skillet brown meat slowly on all sides in hot shortening. Season with salt and pepper. Remove from heat; add the ½ cup water. Cover tightly, return to heat, and simmer slowly till tender, 2 to 2½ hours. Add water, if needed. Pour off pan juices into measuring cup; skim off fat. Add water, if necessary, to make 1 cup.

In saucepan combine pan juices, condensed beef broth, onion, and Worcestershire. Bring to boiling; reduce heat and simmer 5 minutes. Slice the beef as thinly as possible. Slice the rolls lengthwise, cutting almost all the way through. Place a few of the slices inside each roll. Serve each sandwich with about ⅓ *cup* of the hot broth. Serves 6.

Tomato-Bean Combo

    1 16-ounce can cut green
       beans, drained
    2 medium tomatoes, peeled,
       chopped, and drained
¼ cup finely chopped onion
¼ cup dairy sour cream
¼ cup Italian salad dressing
    Romaine leaves
    Tomato wedges

In a bowl combine drained green beans, chopped tomato, and the onion. Blend together the sour cream and Italian salad dressing; add to the bean mixture and toss lightly. Chill salad at least 2 hours. At serving time, spoon salad into individual romaine-lined salad bowls. Garnish with tomato wedges. Serves 6.

BARBECUE SUPPER

Barbecued Smoked Ribs
Calico Potato Salad
Sliced Tomatoes
Hot Garlic Toast
Ginger-Pineapple Pudding
Lemonade

Special Helps: Everyone likes the tantalizing aroma of sizzling meat cooked over the coals, so get out the grill and have a barbecue. While Hubby's watching the ribs, you can put together the salad and fix the dessert. The children can butter the bread slices and set the table.

Calico Potato Salad

    7 medium potatoes, cooked,
       peeled, and diced
    ½ cup diced cucumber
    ½ cup chopped onion
    ¼ cup chopped green pepper
    3 tablespoons chopped
       canned pimiento
  1 ½ teaspoons salt
    ¾ teaspoon celery seed
    2 hard-cooked eggs
    ⅓ cup mayonnaise *or* salad
       dressing
    3 tablespoons vinegar
    2 tablespoons sugar
    1 tablespoon prepared mustard
    ½ cup whipping cream
       Lettuce

Stir together potatoes, cucumber, onion, green pepper, pimiento, salt, celery seed, and ¼ teaspoon pepper. Reserve 1 egg yolk. Coarsely chop the white and remaining egg. Add chopped eggs to potato mixture; chill. Blend mayonnaise, vinegar, sugar, and mustard; whip cream and fold into mayonnaise mixture. One-half hour before serving, toss with potato mixture. To serve, spoon into lettuce-lined bowl. Sieve reserved yolk over salad. Serves 6.

Barbecued Smoked Ribs

In saucepan combine 1 cup smoke-flavored barbecue sauce, ¼ cup catsup, ¼ cup sorghum *or* dark molasses, ¼ cup butter *or* margarine, 2 tablespoons vinegar, 2 tablespoons lemon juice, 2 teaspoons Worcestershire sauce, 1 teaspoon dry mustard, and ½ teaspoon bottled hot pepper sauce. Simmer mixture for 10 minutes.

Place hickory chips in water to soak. Place *slow* coals on both sides of drip pan. Place 4 pounds pork loin back ribs, bone side down, on grill over drip pan. Add damp hickory chips to *slow* coals; lower smoke hood. Barbecue ribs over *slow* coals for 2 to 2½ hours, basting both sides of ribs with sauce the last 30 minutes of cooking. Makes 4 servings.

Ginger-Pineapple Pudding

    1 8¼-ounce can crushed pineapple
    ¼ cup butter *or* margarine
    ¼ cup packed brown sugar
    1 teaspoon vanilla
    2 egg yolks
    2 cups finely crushed gingersnaps
       (30 cookies)
    1 teaspoon baking powder
    ¼ teaspoon salt
    1 5⅓-ounce can evaporated milk
    2 stiffly beaten egg whites
       Pineapple Sauce

Drain pineapple, reserving syrup. In large mixing bowl cream together butter, brown sugar, and vanilla till fluffy. Add egg yolks; beat well. Mix together gingersnap crumbs, baking powder, and salt. Add to creamed mixture alternately with evaporated milk; mix well after each addition. Stir in drained pineapple.

Fold in beaten egg whites. Turn mixture into greased 9-inch pie plate. Baked, uncovered, at 325° for 30 to 35 minutes. Serve warm with Pineapple Sauce. Makes 6 servings.

Pineapple Sauce: To reserved pineapple syrup, add enough water to make ¾ cup. In small saucepan combine ¼ cup sugar and 1 tablespoon cornstarch; stir in syrup mixture. Cook and stir till thickened and bubbly. Stir in 1 tablespoon lemon juice and a few drops of the yellow food coloring, if desired. Serve sauce hot over warm pudding. Makes ¾ cup.

Recipes-Plain and Fancy

Poached Halibut Steaks

- 4 frozen halibut steaks
- 2 tablespoons chopped onion
- 2 tablespoons chopped green pepper
- 1 tablespoon butter *or* margarine
- 1 teaspoon cornstarch
- 1 teaspoon sugar
  Dash garlic salt
- 1 8-ounce can tomatoes, cut up
- 2 tablespoons sliced pimiento-stuffed green olives
- 1 tablespoon prepared horseradish

Put frozen steaks in skillet with just enough water to cover. Add ¾ teaspoon salt; bring to boiling. Reduce heat; cover and simmer till fish flakes easily when tested with fork, 7 to 8 minutes. Thoroughly drain fish.

Meanwhile, in small saucepan cook onion and green pepper in butter till tender but not brown. Blend in cornstarch, sugar, garlic salt, and dash pepper. Stir in undrained tomatoes, olives, and horseradish. Cook and stir until thickened and bubbly. Serve over fish. Serves 4.

Chicken-Fruit Sandwiches

- 12 slices white bread
  Butter *or* margarine, softened
- 1 8¼-ounce can crushed pineapple
- 1 3-ounce package cream cheese, softened
- 2 cups finely chopped cooked chicken *or* turkey
- 2 tablespoons snipped parsley
- ½ teaspoon salt
  Lettuce leaves

Spread one side of each slice of bread with butter. Drain pineapple, reserving 2 to 3 tablespoons syrup. Beat cheese and reserved syrup together. Stir in chicken, pineapple, parsley, and salt; spread on buttered side of *6 slices*. Arrange lettuce atop. Top with remaining bread, buttered side down. Makes 6.

Sausage-Sauerbraten Burgers

- 1 beaten egg
- 1 pound bulk pork sausage
- ¼ pound ground beef
- ¼ cup chopped onion
- 1 cup dry red wine
- ¼ cup vinegar
- 2 tablespoons sugar
- 1 bay leaf, crushed
- ¼ teaspoon ground ginger
- 4 teaspoons cornstarch
- 6 hamburger buns, split and buttered
- 6 thin slices onion

Combine egg, sausage, beef, onion, and ½ teaspoon salt. Shape into 6 patties. Brown the patties on both sides; remove from skillet and set aside. Drain off fat. Combine wine, vinegar, sugar, bay leaf, and ginger. In same skillet bring ½ *cup* of the wine mixture to boiling.

Return patties to pan; cook, covered, 10 minutes. Remove patties from skillet; keep warm. Slowly blend remaining wine mixture with cornstarch. Add to liquid in skillet. Cook and stir till thickened. Place one meat patty on bottom of each bun. Top each with an onion slice and bun top. Serve with sauce. Makes 6.

Tiny Ham Pizza Muffins

- 4 English muffins, split and toasted
- 1 8-ounce can tomato sauce with onion
  Dried oregano, crushed
- ½ medium green pepper
- 1 cup diced fully cooked ham
- 1 cup shredded mozzarella cheese

Spread each muffin half with tomato sauce; sprinkle with the oregano. Thinly slice green pepper into 8 rings. Top each muffin half with some of the ham and a green pepper ring. Sprinkle with cheese. Place muffins on baking sheet. Broil 4 inches from the heat till cheese is melted, about 4 minutes. Makes 8.

Serve hearty *Taco Burgers* with corn chips for a great-tasting light lunch. Layer a well-seasoned ground beef and tomato filling, lettuce, and shredded American cheese atop a toasted hamburger bun. Furnish a knife and fork so you will be sure not to lose any of the taco.

Taco Burgers

     1 pound ground beef
     1 16-ounce can tomatoes, cut up
     1 teaspoon chili powder
     1 teaspoon Worcestershire sauce
    ¾ teaspoon garlic salt
    ½ teaspoon sugar
    ¼ teaspoon dry mustard
     8 hamburger buns, split
       and toasted
     2 cups shredded lettuce
     1 cup shredded American cheese
       (4 ounces)

In skillet brown the meat; drain off fat. Add undrained tomatoes, chili powder, Worcestershire sauce, garlic salt, sugar, and dry mustard. Stir well, breaking up large pieces of tomato. Bring to boiling; reduce heat. Boil gently, uncovered, till thick, 15 to 20 minutes. Spoon onto toasted buns. Sprinkle each of the burgers with lettuce and shredded cheese. Makes 8.

Chicken-Deviled Ham Sandwiches

     8 slices white bread, toasted
     1 4½-ounce can deviled ham
    ⅓ cup mayonnaise *or* salad
       dressing
     1 teaspoon lemon juice
    ½ teaspoon salt
    ⅛ teaspoon pepper
    1½ cups finely chopped cooked
       chicken
    ½ cup chopped celery
       Lettuce
       Cherry tomatoes

Spread one side of each slice of toast with deviled ham. Combine mayonnaise, lemon juice, salt, and pepper. Stir in chicken and celery. Spread chicken mixture over *four* of the bread slices. Top with lettuce and remaining bread slices, ham side down. Halve sandwiches. Garnish each sandwich half with a tomato secured with a pick. Makes 4.

Salmon en Croute

1 13¾-ounce package hot roll mix
1 teaspoon dried dillweed
2 16-ounce cans salmon, drained
    and finely flaked
1 cup soft bread crumbs
2 beaten eggs
1 tablespoon lemon juice
    Peas in Cheese Sauce

Prepare dough from the hot roll mix according to package directions, adding dillweed to the dry ingredients. Let rise in warm place till double (30 to 45 minutes). On well-floured surface, roll dough to an 18-inch circle. Gently fit it into a 6½-cup ring mold, allowing the dough to cover center and hang over edges. Lightly stir together the salmon, bread crumbs, eggs, lemon juice, 1 teaspoon salt, and dash pepper till combined. Spoon salmon filling into mold. Bring dough from sides over top of filling, seal dough at rim of center hole. Cut an X in the dough covering the hole; fold the 4 triangles back over top of ring, sealing to outer edges. Let rise till almost double (30 to 45 minutes). Bake at 325° for 45 to 50 minutes. Cover with foil last 20 minutes. Cool 10 minutes; turn out on platter. Serve with Peas in Cheese Sauce. Serves 8.

Peas in Cheese Sauce: Melt 3 tablespoons butter; blend in 3 tablespoons all-purpose flour, ¾ teaspoon salt, and dash pepper. Add 1½ cups milk all at once; cook and stir till thickened and bubbly. Stir in ½ cup shredded American cheese; one 10-ounce package frozen peas, cooked and drained; and 1 tablespoon lemon juice. Heat and stir till cheese melts and the sauce is hot. Makes 3½ cups.

Seafood Amandine

Prepare one 6-ounce package noodles with chicken sauce mix and almonds according to package directions, reserving the almonds. Stir in one 7½-ounce can minced clams, drained; one 4½-ounce can shrimp, drained; and one 3-ounce can sliced mushrooms, drained.

Turn into a 1½-quart casserole. Sprinkle with 2 tablespoons grated Parmesan cheese, 2 tablespoons snipped parsley, and reserved almonds. Bake at 375° for 40 minutes. Serves 6.

Estofado

1 pound beef stew meat, cut in
    1-inch cubes
1 tablespoon cooking oil
1 cup dry red wine
1 8-ounce can tomatoes
1 large onion, sliced ¼ inch
    thick
1 green pepper, cut in strips
¼ cup raisins
¼ cup dried apricots, halved
1 clove garlic, minced
    Bouquet Garni
½ cup sliced fresh mushrooms
¼ cup sliced ripe olives
1 tablespoon all-purpose flour
    Hot cooked rice

Brown the meat in hot oil. Stir in next seven ingredients, 1½ teaspoons salt, and ⅛ teaspoon pepper. Add Bouquet Garni. Simmer, covered, 1 hour. Stir in mushrooms and olives; simmer 30 minutes more. Discard Bouquet Garni. Blend 1 cup cold water slowly into flour; stir into stew. Cook, stirring constantly, till mixture bubbles. Serve over rice. Makes 6 servings.

Bouquet Garni: Tie 1 teaspoon dried basil, 1 teaspoon dried thyme, 1 teaspoon dried tarragon, and 1 bay leaf in cheesecloth.

Glazed Turkey Roast
Colorful plum-glazed roast shown on the cover—

1 2½-pound frozen boneless
    turkey roast
1 cup plum preserves
½ cup Italian salad dressing
½ envelope onion soup mix
1 tablespoon cornstarch

Remove roast from foil pan; wrap in heavy foil. Place in shallow roasting pan and roast at 350° for 2 hours. Combine preserves, salad dressing, and soup mix. Loosen foil; pour preserve mixture over turkey, then reseal. Insert meat thermometer. Roast till meat thermometer registers 185°, 1¾ to 2 hours more.

Transfer roast to plate; reserve drippings. Blend 2 tablespoons cold water slowly into cornstarch; stir into drippings. Cook and stir till thickened. Spoon some of the sauce over turkey; pass remaining. Serves 8 to 10.

Wheat-Coated Chicken

Place ⅓ cup crushed shredded wheat biscuit, 3 tablespoons dry cream of wheat, 1 tablespoon all-purpose flour, 1 teaspoon sugar, 1 teaspoon paprika, ¾ teaspoon salt, and ¼ teaspoon pepper in plastic or paper bag. Close bag and shake to mix. Dip 4 large ready-to-cook chicken legs and 4 large ready-to-cook chicken thighs in milk. Shake chicken in wheat mixture, one piece at a time, till well coated.

Place on rack; let dry about 20 minutes. Heat ¼ inch of cooking oil in large, heavy skillet. Brown chicken slowly in hot oil 15 minutes. Reduce heat; cover. Cook over low heat, 30 to 40 minutes. Uncover last 10 minutes to crisp chicken. Remove to warm platter. Serve with Cream Gravy. Serves 4.

Cream Gravy: Discard all but *3 tablespoons* of the drippings in skillet. Blend 3 tablespoons all-purpose flour into drippings. Add 1½ cups milk, ½ teaspoon salt, and dash pepper. Cook and stir till thickened and bubbly. Cook 1 to 2 minutes more. Makes 1½ cups gravy.

Dilly Stroganoff

  1 pound ground beef
  1 cup chopped onion
  1 cup fresh mushrooms, sliced
  1 clove garlic, minced
  ¾ cup beef broth
  ½ cup dry red wine
  ¼ cup catsup
  2 tablespoons snipped parsley
  ½ teaspoon dried dillweed
  ½ teaspoon salt
    Dash pepper
  1 cup dairy sour cream
  1 tablespoon all-purpose flour
  8 ounces medium noodles,
    cooked and drained
    Grated Parmesan cheese

Cook beef, onion, mushrooms, and garlic till meat is browned and vegetables are tender. Drain off fat. Stir in broth, wine, catsup, parsley, dillweed, salt, and pepper. Cover; simmer 10 minutes. Blend together sour cream and flour; stir into beef mixture. Cook and stir till thickened (do not boil). Add noodles; heat through. Sprinkle with cheese. Serves 6.

Beer-Braised Rabbit

  1 2-pound ready-to-cook rabbit,
    cut up
  3 tablespoons cooking oil
  3 potatoes, peeled and halved
  3 to 4 carrots, bias-cut in
    1-inch pieces
  1 onion, sliced
  1 cup beer
  ¼ cup chili sauce
  1 tablespoon packed brown sugar
  1 clove garlic, minced
  3 tablespoons all-purpose flour

Season rabbit generously with salt and pepper. In Dutch oven brown the rabbit in hot oil. Add potatoes, carrots, and onion. Combine beer, chili sauce, brown sugar, and garlic; pour over rabbit. Cover; simmer till tender, about 1 hour. Remove meat and vegetables to warm serving platter. Measure pan juices, and add more beer or water, if necessary, to make 1½ cups. Return juices to Dutch oven. Blend ⅓ cup cold water into the flour and ½ teaspoon salt; stir into pan juices. Cook and stir till thickened. Return to gravy; heat through. Serves 4.

Spanish-Style Round Steak

  1½ pounds beef round steak,
    cut ¾ inch thick
  2 tablespoons cooking oil
  ½ cup chopped onion
  1 clove garlic, minced
  1 12-ounce can vegetable juice
    cocktail (1½ cups)
  1 10½-ounce can condensed
    beef broth (1⅓ cups)
  1⅓ cups long grain rice
  1 10-ounce package frozen peas
  ¼ cup chopped canned pimiento

Cut round steak in ¼-inch strips; sprinkle with 1½ teaspoons salt and ¼ teaspoon pepper. In skillet brown half of the strips at a time in hot oil. Add onion and garlic; cook till onion is tender but not brown. Add vegetable juice, broth, and 1⅓ cups water. Bring to boiling; reduce heat. Cover; cook 30 minutes. Stir in rice, peas, and pimiento. Return to boiling. Reduce heat; cook till meat is tender and rice is done, about 20 minutes more. Serves 6 to 8.

Cheese-Topped Green Beans
Sprinkled with Parmesan and toasted almonds—

- 1 pound green beans
- 1 cup water
- ½ envelope onion soup mix (¼ cup)
- 3 tablespoons butter *or* margarine
- ⅓ cup slivered almonds, toasted
- 3 tablespoons grated Parmesan cheese
- ½ teaspoon paprika

Wash beans; remove ends. Cut beans in 1-inch pieces. In medium saucepan combine the beans, water, and onion soup mix. Bring to boiling; simmer till beans are tender, 15 to 20 minutes. Drain beans. Turn into serving dish; stir in butter till melted. Combine toasted almonds, Parmesan cheese, and paprika; sprinkle over the green beans. Makes 6 to 8 servings.

Cheddar-Squash Bake

- 2 pounds yellow crookneck summer squash
- Salt
- 2 beaten egg yolks
- 1 cup dairy sour cream
- 2 tablespoons all-purpose flour
- 2 stiffly beaten egg whites
- 1½ cups shredded Cheddar cheese (6 ounces)
- 4 slices bacon, crisp-cooked, drained, and crumbled
  • • •
- ⅓ cup fine dry bread crumbs
- 1 tablespoon butter *or* margarine, melted

Scrub squash and trim off ends; do not peel. Slice to make about 6 cups. In covered saucepan cook squash in small amount of boiling salted water till just tender, 15 to 20 minutes. Drain thoroughly; sprinkle with salt. Reserve a few slices of squash for garnish. Combine egg yolks, sour cream, and flour. Fold in egg whites. In 12x7½x2-inch baking dish layer half the squash, egg mixture, and cheese; sprinkle bacon over. Repeat layers. Combine crumbs and butter; sprinkle around edge. Arrange reserved squash atop. Bake at 350° for 20 to 25 minutes. Garnish with bacon curls and parsley sprig, if desired. Makes 8 to 10 servings.

Zucchini Fritters
A two-cheese flavored sauce provides the accent—

- 1½ cups all-purpose flour
- 2 teaspoons baking powder
- ¾ teaspoon salt
- 1 beaten egg
- 1 cup milk
- 1 cup finely chopped zucchini
- Fat for frying
- 2 tablespoons butter *or* margarine
- 2 tablespoons all-purpose flour
- ¼ teaspoon salt
- Dash pepper
- 1¼ cups milk
- ½ cup shredded sharp American cheese (2 ounces)
- ½ cup shredded Swiss cheese (2 ounces)

In mixing bowl stir together 1½ cups flour, baking powder, and ¾ teaspoon salt. Combine egg, 1 cup milk, and zucchini. Add to dry ingredients in mixing bowl; stir just till moistened. Drop batter from tablespoon into deep hot fat. Fry, a few at a time, for 3 to 4 minutes. Drain and keep warm. In saucepan melt butter over low heat. Blend in 2 tablespoons flour, ¼ teaspoon salt, and pepper. Add 1¼ cups milk all at once. Cook and stir till thickened and bubbly. Add cheeses, stirring till melted. Spoon over fritters. Makes 24 fritters.

Marinated Zucchini on Tomatoes

- 1 pound zucchini, thinly sliced (2 cups)
- ½ cup cream-style cottage cheese with chives
- ¼ cup dairy sour cream
- 1 tablespoon lemon juice
- ½ teaspoon garlic salt
- ¼ cup chopped green pepper
- 2 medium tomatoes, sliced
- Endive or parsley

In covered saucepan cook zucchini in small amount of boiling water till crisp-tender, 2 to 3 minutes. Drain well. In mixing bowl combine cottage cheese, sour cream, lemon juice, and garlic salt. Add zucchini and green pepper; toss to coat. Chill. Serve on tomato slices. Garnish with endive. Makes 4 or 5 servings.

Corn and Cabbage Combo

> 3 ears fresh corn *or* 1 10-ounce
>   package frozen whole kernel
>   corn
> 2 cups shredded cabbage
> 2 tablespoons chopped onion
> 2 tablespoons butter *or* margarine
> ½ cup cream-style cottage cheese
> ¼ cup dairy sour cream
> 2 tablespoons grated Parmesan
>   cheese

Remove the husks and silks from ears of corn; rinse. Cut off tips of kernels, holding knife at angle. Scrape cobs with dull edge of knife. In covered saucepan cook corn in small amount of boiling salted water till done, 5 to 8 minutes. (Or, prepare frozen corn according to package directions.) Drain.

In covered saucepan cook cabbage in small amount of boiling salted water till tender, about 7 minutes; drain. In large saucepan cook onion in butter till tender but not brown. Stir in cottage cheese, sour cream, Parmesan, ⅛ teaspoon salt, and ⅛ teaspoon pepper; cook and stir till cottage cheese begins to melt. Combine half the cottage cheese mixture with the corn and the remaining half with the cabbage. Arrange cabbage around outside of skillet; fill center with corn. Heat through. Garnish with green pepper ring and carrot curl in center, if desired. Makes 5 or 6 servings.

Sunshine Carrots

> 7 or 8 medium carrots
> 1 tablespoon sugar
> 1 teaspoon cornstarch
> ¼ teaspoon salt
> ¼ teaspoon ground ginger
> ¼ cup orange juice
> 2 tablespoons butter *or* margarine

Bias-slice carrots crosswise about ½ inch thick. In covered saucepan cook carrots in small amount of boiling salted water till just tender, 15 to 20 minutes; drain. Meanwhile, in small saucepan combine sugar, cornstarch, salt, and ginger. Add orange juice; cook, stirring constantly, till mixture thickens and bubbles. Boil for 1 minute, then stir in butter. Pour over hot carrots, tossing to coat evenly. Serves 6.

Sweet Potatoes in Oranges

> 3 medium oranges, halved
> 1¼ pounds sweet potatoes, cooked,
>   peeled, and mashed
> ¼ cup butter *or* margarine
> 2 eggs
> 2 tablespoons sugar
> ⅛ teaspoon ground cinnamon
> ⅛ teaspoon ground allspice
> 3 marshmallows, halved

Advance preparation: Squeeze juice from orange halves (refrigerate juice to use as desired). Scrape out inside of orange halves. In bowl combine potatoes and butter. Beat in eggs, sugar, cinnamon, and allspice. Season to taste with salt and pepper. Fill orange cups with sweet potato mixture. Place in 11x7½x1½-inch baking pan. Cover; chill till baking time.
Before serving: Uncover the potato-filled oranges and bake at 350° for 35 minutes. Place a marshmallow half on each; continue baking till the marshmallows are lightly browned, 4 to 6 minutes. Makes 6 servings.

Baked Corn with Chive Sauce

Drain two 12-ounce cans whole kernel corn. In a 1-quart casserole combine corn with one 4-ounce container whipped cream cheese with chives, ¼ teaspoon salt, and dash pepper. Cover and bake at 325° about 45 minutes. Serve in sauce dishes. Serves 6.

Easy Potato Pancakes

> 3 cups frozen loose-pack hashed
>   brown potatoes, thawed
> ¼ cup all-purpose flour
> 2 teaspoons seasoned salt
> 1½ teaspoons instant minced onion
> 3 eggs
> ¼ cup milk
> 2 tablespoons cooking oil

In large bowl combine thawed potatoes, flour, salt, onion, and dash pepper. Beat eggs slightly; combine with milk and oil. Stir into potato mixture; let stand 5 minutes. Drop batter by ¼-cup portions onto hot, greased griddle; turn to brown both sides. Makes 10 pancakes.

Tempt hot-weather appetites with chilled plates of *Honeydew Fruit Salad.* Fresh fruits and cubed ham are topped with a peachy yogurt dressing.

While some family members prepare the salad, others can spread date-nut bread with cream cheese for sandwiches to serve alongside.

Honeydew Fruit Salad

    1 honeydew melon
    1 cup cubed fully cooked ham
    1 orange, peeled and sectioned
    ½ cup seedless green grapes,
        halved
    ½ cup fresh dark sweet cherries,
        halved and pitted
    1 large nectarine, chopped
    ¼ cup chopped celery
    ½ cup peach yogurt
    ¼ cup mayonnaise *or*
        salad dressing

Chill all ingredients thoroughly. Cut melon into quarters. Separate melon from shell; cut into pieces, leaving pieces in shell. Combine ham, orange sections, green grapes, cherries, nectarine, and celery. Toss to mix. Spoon the fruit onto melon quarters. Blend peach yogurt and mayonnaise; spoon over fruit mixture on melon. Makes 4 servings.

Sesame Lettuce Salad

    2 tablespoons sesame seed
    ½ cup mayonnaise
    ½ cup French salad dressing
    2 tablespoons grated Parmesan
        cheese
    1 tablespoon sugar
    1 tablespoon vinegar
    1 small head lettuce, torn
    ½ cup chopped green pepper
    2 green onions, sliced
    1 11-ounce can mandarin
        orange sections, drained
    ½ medium cucumber, sliced

In skillet toast sesame seed till lightly browned; set aside. In small bowl combine mayonnaise, French dressing, cheese, sugar, vinegar, toasted sesame seed, and ½ teaspoon salt. Combine lettuce, green pepper, and onion. Add orange sections and cucumber. Pour dressing mixture over; toss lightly. Makes 4 to 6 servings.

Cheesy Coleslaw Mold

    1 3-ounce package lime-flavored
        gelatin
1½ cups boiling water
    2 tablespoons vinegar
    ⅓ cup mayonnaise *or*
        salad dressing
    ½ teaspoon salt
        Dash pepper
1½ cups chopped cabbage
    ½ cup shredded carrot
        (1 medium carrot)
    ½ cup shredded sharp American
        cheese (2 ounces)
    ⅛ teaspoon celery seed
        Lettuce

Advance preparation: Dissolve gelatin in boiling water; stir in vinegar. Combine mayonnaise, salt, and pepper; gradually stir in gelatin mixture. Chill till partially set. Combine chopped cabbage, carrot, cheese, and celery seed. Fold into gelatin mixture. Pour into six to eight ½-cup molds. Chill till firm.
Before serving: Unmold the salads onto lettuce-lined plates. Makes 6 to 8 servings.

Marinated Vegetable Salad

2 cups thinly sliced cucumbers
2 cups thinly sliced carrots
1 cup sliced onion, separated
    into rings
½ cup chopped celery
        • • •
1 cup vinegar
¾ cup sugar
¼ cup salad oil
1 teaspoon celery seed
1 teaspoon salt
¼ teaspoon pepper

Advance preparation: In large bowl combine cucumbers, carrots, onion, and celery. In screw-top jar combine vinegar, sugar, salad oil, celery seed, salt, and pepper; cover and shake vigorously. Pour over vegetables; stir gently. Cover; refrigerate several hours or overnight, stirring occasionally.
Before serving: Drain vegetables; reserve marinade. Return any leftover vegetables to marinade; store in refrigerator. Serves 6 to 8.

Broccoli-Tomato Salad

Advance preparation: Thoroughly wash ½ pound broccoli. Remove flowerets. (Use stalks as desired.) In saucepan cook flowerets in small amount of boiling salted water 3 to 4 minutes. Drain well; cool. In bowl combine 1 cup dairy sour cream, ¼ cup milk, ½ teaspoon curry powder, ¼ teaspoon dry mustard, ¼ teaspoon seasoned salt, and dash pepper. Pour over broccoli flowerets; stir to coat. Chill 2 to 3 hours.
Before serving: Cut 3 medium tomatoes into wedges. Arrange with broccoli on bed of lettuce. Makes 5 or 6 servings.

Cheddar Cheese-Pineapple Salad

1 3-ounce package lemon-flavored
    gelatin
1 cup boiling water
½ cup dairy sour cream
¼ cup mayonnaise
1 13¼-ounce can crushed pineapple
½ cup shredded sharp Cheddar
    cheese (2 ounces)
    Lettuce

In bowl dissolve gelatin in boiling water. Cool slightly, then beat in sour cream and mayonnaise. Stir in *undrained* pineapple; chill till partially set. Fold in cheese. Pour into a 4-cup ring mold. Chill till firm.
    To serve, unmold salad onto lettuce-lined platter. Fill center of ring with additional lettuce, if desired. Makes 6 servings.

Frenchy Vegetable Salad

Advance preparation: Remove and discard green top from one medium celery root (about 1 pound). Peel and dice. Add to small amount of boiling salted water in saucepan. Cover and cook till tender, 20 to 25 minutes; drain. Cut 2 medium carrots into julienne strips to make about 1 cup. Pit and peel 1 large avocado; chop to make about 1⅓ cups. In deep bowl combine vegetables. Pour ⅔ cup French salad dressing over and toss to coat. Refrigerate 2 to 3 hours, stirring occasionally.
Before serving: Drain vegetables lightly and spoon into lettuce cups. Serves 6 to 8.

Individual Italian Rolls

See Pot Roast Dip Sandwiches shown on page 48 —

In large mixing bowl stir together 1½ cups all-purpose flour with 1 package active dry yeast. Combine 1½ cups warm water (110°) and 1½ teaspoons salt. Add to flour in bowl. Beat at low speed of electric mixer for ½ minute, scraping sides of bowl constantly. Beat 3 minutes at high speed. By hand, stir in 1¾ to 2 cups flour to make a very stiff dough. Turn out onto lightly floured surface; knead till smooth (10 minutes). Shape into a ball; place in lightly greased bowl, turning once. Cover; let rise in warm place till double (about 1 hour). Punch down; turn out onto lightly floured surface. Divide in half. Cover; let rest 10 minutes.

Cut each half of dough in thirds, making 6 pieces. Round each to a ball. Cover; let rest 10 minutes. Shape each into a 7-inch loaf, tapering ends. Place 2 to 3 inches apart on greased baking sheet that has been sprinkled with cornmeal. Press down ends of loaves. With sharp knife, make 3 shallow cuts diagonally across top of each loaf. Stir 1 tablespoon water into 1 slightly beaten egg white; brush over top and sides of loaves. Cover; let rise till double (45 to 60 minutes). Place large shallow pan on lower rack of oven; fill with boiling water. Place baking sheet on rack above. Bake at 400° about 15 minutes. Brush again with egg white mixture; bake 5 to 10 minutes more. Cool on wire racks. Makes 6 loaves.

Easy Sugar Cookies

    ¾ cup sugar
    ½ cup shortening
    1 egg
    ½ teaspoon vanilla
    1¼ cups all-purpose flour
    1 teaspoon cream of tartar
    ½ teaspoon baking soda
    ¼ teaspoon salt

Cream together sugar and shortening. Add egg and vanilla; mix well. Combine flour, cream of tartar, soda, and salt; stir into creamed mixture. Form dough into 1-inch balls. Place on ungreased cookie sheet. Top with walnut halves or candied cherries, if desired. Bake at 325° for 14 to 16 minutes. Makes 48.

Sausage Bread

    ½ pound bulk *or* link Italian
        sausage
    3¼ to 3½ cups all-purpose flour
    1 package active dry yeast
    1¼ cups warm water (110°)
    ½ teaspoon salt

Cook sausage over medium heat till done, about 15 minutes; break sausage apart as it cooks. Remove casings from link sausage. Drain well. In mixing bowl stir together *1½ cups* of the flour and yeast. Combine warm water and salt. Add to flour in bowl. Beat at low speed of electric mixer for ½ minute, scraping sides of bowl. Beat 3 minutes at high speed.

By hand, stir in sausage and enough flour to make a moderately stiff dough. Turn onto lightly floured surface; knead till smooth and elastic (8 to 10 minutes). Shape into ball; place in lightly greased bowl. Turn once; cover.

Let rise till double (45 to 60 minutes). Punch down; turn onto lightly floured surface. Cover; let rest 10 minutes. Shape into loaf; place in greased 8½x4½x2½-inch loaf pan. Cover; let rise till double (30 to 45 minutes).

Bake at 400° till done, about 35 minutes. Cover with foil after 20 minutes to prevent over-browning. Remove from pan; cool. Makes 1.

Coconut-Pecan Rounds

    1 cup butter *or* margarine
    ¾ cup granulated sugar
    ¾ cup packed brown sugar
    2 eggs
    1 teaspoon vanilla
    2½ cups all-purpose flour
    1 teaspoon baking powder
    ½ teaspoon salt
    1 cup flaked coconut
    ¾ cup chopped pecans

Cream together butter and sugars. Add eggs, one at a time, blending well after each. Beat in vanilla. Thoroughly combine flour, baking powder, and salt; stir into creamed mixture. Stir in coconut and pecans. Form into 2 rolls, 1½ inches in diameter. Wrap in waxed paper; chill thoroughly. Slice ¼ inch thick and place 2 inches apart on ungreased baking sheet. Bake at 375° for 8 to 10 minutes. Makes 80.

Oatmeal Chippers

Peanuts in a chewy cookie shown on page 48 —

- 1 cup granulated sugar
- 1 cup packed brown sugar
- ½ cup butter *or* margarine, softened
- ½ cup shortening
- 2 eggs
- 1 teaspoon vanilla
- 1½ cups all-purpose flour
- 1 teaspoon baking soda
- 3 cups quick-cooking rolled oats
- 1 6-ounce package semisweet chocolate pieces (1 cup)
- 1 cup coarsely chopped salted peanuts

In large mixing bowl cream together sugars, butter, and shortening till fluffy. Add eggs and vanilla; beat well. Stir together flour and soda. Add to creamed mixture with oats; mix thoroughly. Stir in chocolate pieces and peanuts. Drop from teaspoon, about 2 inches apart, onto ungreased cookie sheet. Bake at 375° for 10 to 12 minutes. Makes 72.

Feather Brownies

- 1 cup sugar
- ½ cup butter, softened
- 2 eggs
- ⅓ cup water
- 1 teaspoon vanilla
- ½ teaspoon red food coloring (optional)
- 1 cup all-purpose flour
- ⅓ cup unsweetened cocoa powder
- ½ teaspoon baking powder
- ¼ teaspoon salt
- ⅓ cup chopped nuts

In mixing bowl cream together sugar and butter till fluffy. Separate eggs, reserving whites. Add egg yolks to creamed mixture with water, vanilla, and food coloring; beat well. Thoroughly stir together flour, cocoa powder, baking powder, and salt. Add to creamed mixture; mix well. Stir in nuts. Beat egg whites to stiff peaks; fold into batter. Turn into greased 13x9x2-inch baking pan. Bake at 350° for 20 to 25 minutes. Cool. Sprinkle with powdered sugar, if desired. Cut into bars. Makes 36.

Frosted Date Bars

- 1 cup finely chopped pitted dates
- 1 egg
- ½ cup packed brown sugar
- ½ cup butter
- ¼ cup milk
- 1¼ cups all-purpose flour
- ½ teaspoon salt
- ½ teaspoon baking powder
- ¼ teaspoon baking soda
- ½ cup chopped nuts
- 1 cup sifted powdered sugar
- 2 tablespoons butter, softened
- ½ teaspoon vanilla
- Milk

Bring dates and ½ cup water to boiling. Simmer 5 minutes; cool. Reserve 2 tablespoons for frosting. In bowl combine remaining dates with egg, brown sugar, ½ cup butter, and ¼ cup milk; beat well. Stir together flour, salt, baking powder, and soda; beat into egg mixture. Stir in nuts. Spread in greased 9x9x2-inch baking pan. Bake at 350° about 25 minutes.

Meanwhile, combine powdered sugar, 2 tablespoons butter, vanilla, and reserved dates; beat well. Add milk to make of spreading consistency. Spread frosting atop slightly warm cookies. Cool thoroughly; cut. Makes 24.

Chewy Apricot Bars

- ¾ cup finely snipped dried apricots
- ½ cup butter *or* margarine, melted
- 1½ cups packed brown sugar
- 2 eggs
- 1 teaspoon vanilla
- 2 cups all-purpose flour
- 2 teaspoons baking powder
- ¾ teaspoon ground cinnamon
- ¼ teaspoon salt
- ½ cup chopped pecans

Pour boiling water over apricots; cool 10 minutes. Drain well. In saucepan melt butter; remove from heat. Stir in sugar. Beat in eggs and vanilla. Combine flour, baking powder, cinnamon, and salt. Blend into butter mixture. Stir in apricots and pecans. Spread in greased 13x9x2-inch baking pan. Bake at 350° for 30 to 35 minutes. Cut in bars while warm. Makes 36.

Dessert-in-a-mug describes *Cran-Raspberry Float.* Pour cranberry juice over a raspberry sherbet-filled mug; top with lemon sherbet.

Nectarines Royale is an elegant dessert-in-a-dish. Chill fresh fruit slices in a brandy syrup and serve them with sour cream topping.

Cran-Raspberry Float

Using 1 pint raspberry sherbet, fill each of 4 tall glasses with spoonfuls of sherbet. Pour ¾ *cup* chilled cranberry juice cocktail into *each* glass. Using one 12-ounce bottle chilled lemon-lime carbonated beverage, carefully fill glasses. Stir gently. Top each with a scoop of lemon sherbet; garnish with mint. Serves 4.

Strawberry-Peach-Brandy Float

Thaw one 10-ounce package frozen strawberries enough to cut into cubes. Place in blender container. Pour in one 12-ounce can peach nectar (1½ cups) and ⅓ cup peach brandy. Cover and blend well. Add 1 pint lemon sherbet, a scoop at a time, blending just a few seconds after each addition. Pour into chilled glasses. Top with additional scoops of sherbet. Garnish with mint. Makes 4 cups.

Nectarines Royale

        6 medium nectarines
            (1½ pounds)
        1 cup granulated sugar
        1 cup water
        3 tablespoons brandy
    1½ teaspoons vanilla
        ½ cup dairy sour cream
        2 tablespoons powdered sugar
        1 tablespoon brandy

Place nectarines in boiling water to loosen peel. Remove peel; pit and cut in quarters. In large saucepan combine nectarines, granulated sugar, and water. Bring to boiling; simmer 1 minute. Stir in 3 tablespoons brandy and vanilla. Let stand till fruit reaches room temperature, then chill. Just before serving, arrange fruit in six individual dessert dishes. Combine sour cream, powdered sugar, and 1 tablespoon brandy. Spoon over nectarines. Makes 6 servings.

Coffeescotch Pudding
Toasted spiced crumbs are the crunchy topping —

1 3¾- or 4-ounce package
   regular butterscotch
   pudding mix
2 teaspoons instant coffee
   crystals
½ cup soft bread crumbs
1 tablespoon sugar
1 tablespoon butter *or* margarine
   Dash ground cinnamon

In a saucepan combine pudding mix and coffee crystals. Prepare pudding mix according to the package directions. Pour into 4 dessert dishes. Chill in refrigerator until serving time. In small skillet combine the bread crumbs, sugar, butter, and cinnamon. Cook and stir over low heat till crumbs are browned and crisp. Set aside. Just before serving, sprinkle crumbs over pudding. Makes 4 servings.

Tangerine-Coconut Freeze
An easy-to-make treat with a sunny citrus flavor —

1 cup flaked coconut
1 3- or 3¼-ounce package *regular*
   vanilla pudding mix
3 cups milk
2 cups light cream
1 6-ounce can frozen tangerine
   juice concentrate, thawed
¾ cup light corn syrup
1 teaspoon vanilla
3 drops red food coloring
2 drops yellow food coloring

Spread coconut in a shallow baking pan. Toast at 350° till lightly brown, 6 to 7 minutes. Shake pan or stir often to ensure even toasting; set aside. (Toast additional coconut for garnish, if desired.)

Pour pudding mix into saucepan; gradually stir in 2 cups of the milk. Cook and stir over medium heat till thickened and bubbly; cool. Blend in remaining milk, cream, toasted coconut, tangerine juice concentrate, corn syrup, vanilla, and the two food colorings.

Freeze in 4-quart ice cream freezer following manufacturer's directions. Let ripen. Sprinkle each serving with additional toasted coconut, if desired. Makes 3 quarts.

Butterscotch Party Torte

1 6-ounce package butterscotch
   pieces (1 cup)
¾ cup sugar
½ cup butter *or* margarine
3 eggs
2¼ cups all-purpose flour
1½ teaspoons baking powder
½ teaspoon baking soda
½ teaspoon salt
1 cup buttermilk
   Coconut-Pecan Filling
½ cup whipping cream

In saucepan combine ⅔ cup of the butterscotch pieces with ¼ cup water. (Reserve remaining pieces for filling.) Heat and stir till pieces melt; set aside. In mixing bowl cream together sugar and butter till fluffy. Add eggs one at a time; beat well after each. Beat in butterscotch mixture. Combine flour, baking powder, soda, and salt. Add to creamed mixture alternately with buttermilk, beating just till blended after each addition. Pour into 2 greased and floured 9x1½-inch round baking pans. Bake at 375° for 25 to 30 minutes; cool. Assemble cake layers with Coconut-Pecan Filling. Before serving, whip cream; frost sides of cake.

Coconut-Pecan Filling: In saucepan blend ½ cup sugar and 1 tablespoon cornstarch. Stir in one 5⅓-ounce can evaporated milk (⅔ cup). Cook and stir over medium heat till thickened and bubbly. Remove from heat. Stir in reserved butterscotch pieces and 2 tablespoons butter *or* margarine. Add 1 cup flaked coconut and ½ cup chopped pecans. Spread half atop each layer.

Lemon Pound Cake

In bowl beat 4 eggs till thick. Add one package 2-layer-size yellow cake mix, one 3¾-ounce package *instant* lemon pudding mix, ¾ cup water, and ⅓ cup cooking oil. Beat 5 minutes at medium speed of electric mixer.

Pour into ungreased 10-inch tube pan with removable bottom. Bake at 350° for 50 minutes. Leave cake on pan bottom; remove sides. Cool 20 to 30 minutes. Remove bottom. Prick top of cake with 2-tined fork. Mix 1 cup sifted powdered sugar and 3 tablespoons lemon juice; heat to boiling. Drizzle over cake.

Meals that Save Dollars

The budget recipes shown here are—(back) Pickled Onion Rings and Carrots, Shrimp-Stuffed Peppers; (center) Sweet-Sour Coleslaw, Banana Bread Pudding; (front) Broccoli and Ham Sauce on Cheese Biscuits, Ruby Poached Apples. (See index for recipe pages.)

Budget-Stretching Menus

LOW-COST LUNCH

Cheesy Tuna Patties
Cottage Cheese
Asparagus Spears   Tomato Wedges
Rye Rolls
or
Honey-Cracked Wheat Bread
(see recipe, page 80)
Fruit Pie
Coffee   Milk

Special Helps: Besides being a good buy, tuna and your own garden-fresh vegetables continue as an all-time family favorite. Give the tuna patties added nutrition at a low cost with nonfat dry milk powder. Before baking the patties, coat each with crushed cheese crackers for a tasty and attractive texture.

Cheesy Tuna Patties

In saucepan cook ¼ cup finely chopped celery in 3 tablespoons butter *or* margarine till tender. Combine ⅓ cup nonfat dry milk powder, 3 tablespoons all-purpose flour, ¼ teaspoon salt, and ¼ teaspoon paprika; blend into the celery mixture. Stir in ¾ cup water. Cook and stir till mixture thickens and bubbles. Remove from heat and cool slightly.

Stir in 2 cups soft bread crumbs (2½ slices); one 6½-ounce can tuna, drained and flaked; and 2 tablespoons chopped green onion. Mix well. Form tuna mixture into six 2½-inch patties, using about ⅓ cup for each. Beat 1 egg and 1 tablespoon water together. Dip patties in egg mixture, then in ⅔ cup finely crushed round cheese crackers (about 16).

Place the patties on greased baking sheet. Bake at 350° for 20 to 25 minutes. Makes 6.

Rye Rolls

4¼ to 4½ cups all-purpose flour
2 packages active dry yeast
2 teaspoons caraway seed
2½ cups warm water (110°)
1 tablespoon salt
3 cups rye flour
Yellow cornmeal
1 slightly beaten egg white

In large mixing bowl combine *3 cups* of the all-purpose flour, yeast, and caraway seed. Combine warm water and salt. Add to dry mixture in mixing bowl. Beat at low speed of electric mixer for ½ minute, scraping bowl constantly.

Beat 3 minutes at high speed. By hand, stir in rye flour and enough of the remaining all-purpose flour to make a stiff dough.

Turn out on lightly floured surface and knead till smooth and elastic (10 to 15 minutes). Shape into a ball. Place in lightly greased bowl; turn once. Cover; let dough rise in warm place till double (45 to 60 minutes).

Punch the dough down; turn out on a lightly floured surface. Divide dough in half. Cover; let rest 10 minutes. Divide each half of the dough in eighths, making 16 pieces in all. Shape each piece into an oval or round roll. Place the rolls about 2 inches apart on a greased baking sheet sprinkled with the cornmeal. With sharp knife, cut a shallow gash in top of each roll. Add 1 tablespoon water to egg white; brush over tops and sides of rolls.

Cover; let rise till double (30 minutes). Place large, shallow pan on lower rack of oven and pour boiling water to depth of 1-inch. Place rolls on baking sheet on rack over water. Bake at 400° about 15 minutes. Brush again with egg white mixture. Bake 10 to 12 minutes longer. Cool on rack. Makes 16 rolls.

Give your family a choice of crusty *Rye Rolls* or *Honey-Cracked Wheat Bread* (see recipe, page 80) to accompany this money-saving meal. Arrange the garden-fresh vegetables with *Cheesy Tuna Patties* for an eye-pleasing main dish.

DINNER FOR SIX

Island Sweet-Sour Meatballs
(see photo, page 4)
Rice
Tossed Green Salad
with
Zippy Celery Seed Dressing
Hard Rolls   Butter
Strawberry Shortcake
Coffee   Green Tea

Special Helps: Soy-based products, such as textured vegetable protein, can save you money because when they are added to ground meat they increase the meat volume by as much as half.

Textured vegetable protein is marketed in two ways — already mixed with ground meat at your meat counter or in a granular form ready to blend with meat. For the homemade mixture, use a pound of ground meat and add the soy product with the amount of liquid specified in the label directions to yield about 1½ pounds.

Strawberry Shortcake

      2 cups all-purpose flour
      3 tablespoons sugar
      1 tablespoon baking powder
      ½ teaspoon salt
      ½ cup shortening
      ⅔ cup milk
        Strawberries, sliced and
          lightly sweetened
        Whipped dessert topping

In bowl stir together flour, sugar, baking powder, and salt. Cut shortening into dry ingredients till mixture resembles coarse crumbs. Add milk; mix vigorously. Knead gently 8 to 10 times on floured surface. Roll ½ inch thick. Cut into 8 biscuits with floured 2½-inch round cutter. Bake on ungreased baking sheet at 450° for 10 minutes. Split warm biscuits; fill and top with berries and topping. Makes 8 servings.

Island Sweet-Sour Meatballs

      1 beaten egg
      1 cup soft bread crumbs
      2 tablespoons chopped onion
      2 tablespoons milk
      1 pound ground beef-textured
          vegetable protein mixture
      2 tablespoons shortening
      1 8¼-ounce can pineapple tidbits
      1 8-ounce can whole cranberry
          sauce (1 cup)
      ½ cup bottled barbecue sauce
      1 tablespoon cornstarch
      ½ cup green pepper strips
        Hot cooked rice

Combine egg, crumbs, onion, milk, and ¾ teaspoon salt. Add meat mixture; mix well. Shape into 24 one-inch balls (1 tablespoonful each).

In large skillet brown the meatballs in hot shortening. Drain off fat. Drain pineapple, reserving syrup; set pineapple aside. Add water to reserved syrup to make ¾ cup. Combine syrup mixture, cranberry sauce, barbecue sauce, ¼ teaspoon salt, and dash pepper. Pour over meatballs in skillet. Bring to boiling. Reduce heat; cover and simmer 15 to 20 minutes. Blend ¼ cup cold water slowly into cornstarch. Stir into skillet. Cook and stir till thickened and bubbly. Add pineapple and green pepper. Simmer, covered, till pepper is barely tender. Serve over rice. Makes 6 servings.

Zippy Celery Seed Dressing

      ⅓ cup salad oil
      3 tablespoons vinegar
      2 tablespoons water
      2 tablespoons chopped onion
      2 tablespoons snipped parsley
      1 teaspoon sugar
      ¾ teaspoon celery seed
      ½ teaspoon dry mustard
      ½ teaspoon salt
      ⅛ teaspoon cayenne
        Salad greens

Combine all ingredients, except greens, in a screw-top jar. Shake to blend well. Cover; store in refrigerator several hours or overnight. Shake before using. Before serving, toss with salad greens. Makes 1 cup.

CASSEROLE SUPPER

Savory Heart and Stuffing
Spanish Citrus Salad
French Bread   Butter
Peanut Butter Cream Torte
Coffee   Tea

Special Helps: Low, moist heat is the answer to making low-cost, less-tender cuts of meat delicious. Also, with variety meats, you don't pay for bone waste.

Peanut Butter Cream Torte

     Pastry for 1-crust 9-inch pie
2¾ **cups milk**
  1 **4½- or 5-ounce package** *regular*
     vanilla pudding mix
  3 **beaten egg yolks**
 ⅓ **cup peanut butter**
 ½ **cup sifted powdered sugar**
  3 **egg whites**
 ½ **teaspoon vanilla**
 ¼ **teaspoon cream of tartar**
 ⅓ **cup granulated sugar**

Remove the bottom from an 8-inch springform pan. Roll and cut pastry to fit ¼ inch over edge of bottom. Prick well with fork. Place on baking sheet. Bake at 450° 10 to 12 minutes; cool. In saucepan gradually stir milk into pudding mix; stir in egg yolks. Cook and stir over medium heat till mixture comes to boil. Remove from heat. Cover surface of pudding with clear plastic wrap; cool.

Cut peanut butter into powdered sugar till crumbly. Carefully assemble sides and bottom of springform pan. Pat peanut butter mixture atop pastry in pan. Spread cooled pudding over peanut butter mixture; chill thoroughly.

Remove sides of springform pan. Beat egg whites with vanilla and cream of tartar till soft peaks form. Gradually add granulated sugar; beat till stiff peaks form. Spread meringue atop, sealing edges. Bake at 400° for 10 minutes. Chill before serving. Serves 8.

Savory Heart and Stuffing

1½ **pounds beef heart**
  1 **13¾-ounce can chicken broth**
  1 **bay leaf**
  1 **cup chopped celery**
 ¼ **cup chopped onion**
  3 **tablespoons butter** *or* **margarine**
  4 **cups coarsely crumbled**
     corn bread *or* **Golden Corn**
     Bread (see recipe, page 80)
  2 **cups dry bread cubes**
     (4 slices bread)
  1 **10-ounce package frozen**
     mixed vegetables, cooked
     and drained
  1 **teaspoon ground sage**
 ½ **teaspoon salt**
  1 **10½-ounce can condensed**
     golden mushroom soup

Slit heart open; remove hard parts from center. Place heart in Dutch oven. Add chicken broth and bay leaf. Cover and simmer till meat is tender, about 2½ hours. Meanwhile, cook celery and onion in butter till tender.

In large bowl combine corn bread crumbs, the bread cubes, mixed vegetables, celery mixture, sage, and salt. Drain heart, reserving 1 cup liquid. Discard bay leaf. Add reserved liquid to corn bread mixture; mix well. Turn into 12x7½x2-inch baking dish. Slice heart and place atop stuffing. Combine mushroom soup and ¼ cup water. Spoon over heart slices. Cover; bake at 350° for 45 minutes. Garnish with parsley, if desired. Serves 8.

Spanish Citrus Salad

Peel and section 3 large oranges; measure 1½ cups. Cut the sections in half crosswise. In large bowl combine the oranges; one 15-ounce can red kidney beans, drained; ½ cup chopped celery; 1 small onion, sliced and separated into rings; and 1 tablespoon snipped parsley.

Blend together ⅓ cup unsweetened grapefruit juice; ¼ cup salad oil; 1 tablespoon vinegar; ½ teaspoon salt; ¼ teaspoon dried oregano, crushed; and ⅛ teaspoon dried thyme, crushed. Pour over mixture in bowl. Chill several hours; stir several times. Serve in lettuce-lined salad bowl. Makes 8 servings.

More-For-Your Money Recipes

Thrifty Bologna-Bean Chowder

    1 cup large dry lima beans
    4 cups water
    1 envelope onion soup mix
    1 teaspoon instant chicken
        bouillon granules
            • • •
    1 16-ounce can tomatoes, cut up
    4 ounces chunk bologna,
        coarsely chopped (1 cup)
    1 cup milk

Rinse beans. Place in large saucepan and add water. Soak overnight. (Or, bring beans to boiling; reduce heat and simmer 2 minutes. Remove from heat. Cover; let stand 1 hour.) Do not drain. Add dry soup mix and chicken bouillon granules. Bring to boiling. Reduce heat and simmer, covered, till beans are tender, about 1¼ hours. Add the undrained tomatoes, bologna, and milk. Heat through, stirring occasionally. Makes 4 servings.

Bronco Buster Soup

    1¼ cups dry pinto beans
    6 cups water
    1 1-pound beef shank
    1 cup chopped onion
    2 teaspoons salt
    ½ teaspoon dried thyme, crushed
    2 medium potatoes, peeled
        and diced (2 cups)
    2 medium carrots, sliced (1 cup)

Rinse beans. Place in large saucepan and add 6 cups water. Soak overnight. (Or, bring beans to boiling; reduce heat and simmer 2 minutes. Remove from heat. Cover; let stand 1 hour.) Do not drain. Add beef shank, onion, salt, thyme, and dash pepper. Bring mixture to boiling. Reduce heat and simmer, covered, 1¼ hours, stirring occasionally. Remove shank; cool. Cut off meat and dice. Discard bones. Mash beans slightly. Add meat, potatoes, and carrots to soup. Cover; simmer the soup 30 minutes more. Makes 6 servings.

Bean Soup and Tamale Dumplings

    2½ cups dry pinto beans
    10 cups water
    4 ounces salt pork, diced
        (1 cup)
    1 cup chopped onion
    1 clove garlic, minced
    1½ teaspoons salt
    1 teaspoon chili powder
    Dash pepper
    Tamale Dumplings

Rinse pinto beans. Place in large saucepan and add water. Soak overnight. (Or, bring beans to boiling; reduce heat and simmer 2 minutes. Remove from heat. Cover; let stand 1 hour.) Do not drain. Add salt pork, chopped onion, garlic, salt, chili powder, and pepper to the beans. Bring to boiling. Reduce heat and simmer, covered, for 1 hour. Remove 1 cup of the bean liquid; set aside to cool. Continue cooking beans till tender, 1½ to 2 hours. Mash the beans slightly.

Drop Tamale Dumplings into simmering beans. Cover tightly; cook 30 minutes more. Serve in soup bowls. Makes 6 to 8 servings.

Tamale Dumplings: In skillet cook ½ pound ground beef and ¼ cup chopped onion till meat is browned and onion is tender. Drain off the excess fat. Stir in 2 teaspoons chili powder, ¼ teaspoon salt, and dash pepper. Set aside to cool. In bowl combine 1½ cups yellow cornmeal, ¾ cup all-purpose flour, 2 teaspoons baking powder, 1 teaspoon salt, and 1 teaspoon sugar. Add the 1 cup cooled bean liquid, stirring till mixture is combined.

Divide the cornmeal mixture into 16 portions. With lightly floured hands, shape each portion around teaspoonful of meat mixture to form a ball. Stir remaining meat into the beans.

Bean Soup and Tamale Dumplings is a cold-weather favorite that won't bruise a budget. Delight your family by ladling up generous servings of steaming soup. A chili-seasoned beef filling is tucked inside each dumpling.

Chicken Chowder

1 envelope tomato-vegetable
   soup mix
3 cups water
1 16-ounce can mixed vegetables
1 15½-ounce can red kidney beans
1 8-ounce can tomatoes, cut up
        • • •
2 5-ounce cans boned chicken,
   cut up

In large saucepan combine dry tomato-vegetable soup mix, water, undrained mixed
vegetables, undrained red kidney beans, and
undrained tomatoes. Heat mixture to boiling.

Reduce heat; simmer, uncovered, for 10
minutes. Stir in the cut-up chicken. Heat mixture through, stirring occasionally. Serves 8.

Shrimp-Stuffed Peppers

This tasty shrimp dish is shown on page 66 —

6 medium green peppers
3 tablespoons butter *or* margarine
3 tablespoons all-purpose flour
1 teaspoon seasoned salt
⅛ teaspoon dried basil, crushed
2 cups milk
¼ teaspoon Worcestershire sauce
½ cup chopped celery
        • • •
1 pound frozen shelled shrimp
3 ounces macaroni, cooked
½ cup shredded American cheese
   (2 ounces)

Cut off tops of green peppers; remove seeds
and membrane. Scallop edges, if desired. Pre-
cook peppers in boiling salted water 5 minutes;
drain. (For crisp peppers, omit precooking.)
Melt butter in skillet; blend in flour, salt,
and basil. Add milk and Worcestershire sauce
all at once; add celery. Cook, stirring constantly, till thickened and bubbly.

Cook shrimp in boiling salted water 1 to
3 minutes; drain and dice. Add shrimp and
macaroni to sauce. Lightly salt inside of peppers. Fill with shrimp mixture; stand upright
in 10x6x2-inch baking dish.

Bake at 350° for 20 to 25 minutes. Sprinkle
cheese atop peppers. Continue baking till the
cheese melts. Makes 6 servings.

Oven-Baked Beef-Lima Stew

1 cup large dry lima beans
¼ cup all-purpose flour
1 8-ounce can tomatoes, cut up
1 cup sliced celery
1 cup sliced carrot
½ cup chopped onion
¼ teaspoon Worcestershire sauce
1 bay leaf
1 pound ground beef

Rinse beans. Place in large saucepan and add
4½ cups water. Soak overnight. (Or, bring
beans to boiling; reduce heat and simmer 2
minutes. Remove from heat. Cover; let stand
1 hour.) Do not drain. Blend ½ cup cold water
slowly into flour. Stir into beans. Return to
heat; cook and stir till bubbly.

Stir in undrained tomatoes, celery, carrot,
onion, Worcestershire, bay leaf, and 1½ teaspoons salt. Crumble ground beef into stew.
Bring mixture to boiling. Cover and bake at
350° for 1½ hours, stirring occasionally.

Remove bay leaf. Skim off excess fat. Season to taste with salt and pepper. Serves 6.

Sausage-Sauced Cabbage

½ pound bulk Italian pork sausage
½ cup chopped onion
½ cup chopped green pepper
1 8-ounce can tomato sauce
1 6-ounce can tomato paste
1 tablespoon snipped parsley
2 teaspoons sugar
1 teaspoon garlic salt
½ teaspoon dried oregano, crushed
1 large head cabbage, cut into
   6 wedges

In saucepan cook sausage, onion, and green
pepper till vegetables are tender. Drain off
excess fat. Stir in tomato sauce, paste, parsley,
sugar, garlic salt, oregano, and 1 cup water.
Cover; simmer 15 minutes, stirring once or
twice. Meanwhile, in a skillet cook cabbage
wedges, covered, in a small amount of boiling
salted water till tender, about 10 minutes.

Remove cabbage from skillet with slotted
spoon; place on rack to drain for a minute or
two. Arrange cabbage on plate. Pour some of
the sauce over and pass remaining. Serves 6.

Instead of serving meat for dinner every night, put yourself in a cost-cutting frame of mind and create a meatless meal—try *Creamy Egg and Noodle Bake*. A tangy sour cream and cheese sauce makes the distinctive green noodles a gourmet delight for you and your family.

Creamy Egg and Noodle Bake

    4 ounces green noodles
        (about 3 cups)
 ½ cup finely chopped onion
    1 clove garlic, minced
    2 tablespoons butter *or* margarine
    8 hard-cooked eggs, chopped
    2 cups small-curd cream-style
        cottage cheese (16 ounces)
    1 cup dairy sour cream
 ⅓ cup grated Parmesan cheese
    2 teaspoons poppy seed
    1 teaspoon Worcestershire sauce
 ½ teaspoon salt
    Dash bottled hot pepper sauce
 ¾ cup soft bread crumbs
        (1 slice bread)
    1 tablespoon butter *or* margarine,
        melted
    Grated Parmesan cheese

In large saucepan cook the noodles in boiling salted water according to package directions. Meanwhile, cook the chopped onion and garlic in the 2 tablespoons butter or margarine till tender but not brown. Thoroughly drain the cooked noodles. Toss noodles with the onion mixture and chopped hard-cooked eggs.

Place the cottage cheese in blender container; cover and blend till smooth. Remove from the blender. Combine cottage cheese, sour cream, the ⅓ cup grated Parmesan cheese, the poppy seed, Worcestershire sauce, salt, bottled hot pepper sauce, and dash pepper. Fold into the noodle mixture.

Turn into 12x7½x2-inch baking dish. Combine the soft bread crumbs and the 1 tablespoon melted butter; sprinkle in a ring atop the casserole. Bake, uncovered, at 350° for 25 minutes. Garnish with additional hardcooked egg quarters, if desired. Pass additional grated Parmesan cheese. Makes 8 servings.

Herbed Spinach Bake

1 10-ounce package frozen
   chopped spinach
2 tablespoons butter *or* margarine
• • •
1 cup cooked rice
1 cup shredded American
   cheese (4 ounces)
⅓ cup milk
2 slightly beaten eggs
2 tablespoons chopped onion
½ teaspoon salt
½ teaspoon Worcestershire sauce
¼ teaspoon dried rosemary,
   crushed

Cook the spinach according to package directions; drain well. Stir in butter till melted. Stir in rice, shredded cheese, milk, eggs, onion, salt, Worcestershire sauce, and rosemary. Pour mixture into ungreased 10x6x2-inch baking dish. Bake at 350° till knife inserted halfway between center and edge comes out clean, 30 to 35 minutes. Cut the spinach into squares to serve. Makes 6 servings.

Barbecued Potatoes and Carrots

4 cups thinly sliced potatoes
1 cup bias-sliced carrot
½ cup shredded sharp American
   cheese (2 ounces)
½ cup chopped celery
¼ cup chopped onion
• • •
1 tablespoon all-purpose flour
1 teaspoon salt
   Dash pepper
⅓ cup hot-style catsup
½ teaspoon Worcestershire sauce
1¾ cups milk

In large bowl combine the potatoes, carrot, shredded cheese, celery, and onion. Combine flour, salt, and pepper; stir into the vegetables, tossing well to coat. Turn mixture into 2-quart casserole. Blend together the hot-style catsup and Worcestershire sauce; gradually stir in milk. Pour over the vegetables.

Cover; bake at 375° for 1¼ hours. Stir through the casserole; bake, uncovered, 15 minutes more. Makes 6 to 8 servings.

Scalloped Zucchini

4 large zucchini (2 pounds)
   Milk
¼ pound bulk pork sausage
¼ cup chopped onion
½ cup finely crushed saltine
   crackers (14 crackers)
¼ cup grated Parmesan cheese
2 slightly beaten eggs
⅛ teaspoon dried thyme, crushed
   Dash garlic salt

Scrub squash and trim off ends; do not peel. Cook whole squash, covered, in small amount of boiling salted water till just tender, 15 minutes. Drain well, reserving ½ cup liquid; add milk to equal ¾ cup and set aside. Chop zucchini coarsely (about 5 cups). In skillet cook sausage and onion together over medium heat till sausage is browned and onion is tender. Drain off excess fat. Stir in squash, milk mixture, crackers, *2 tablespoons* of the cheese, eggs, thyme, garlic salt, ¾ teaspoon salt, and dash pepper; mix well.

Turn mixture into ungreased 10x6x2-inch baking dish; sprinkle with the remaining Parmesan cheese. Bake at 350° till set and delicately browned, about 45 minutes. Serves 8.

Corn-Sauced Onions

6 medium onions, peeled
   and cut in wedges
1 17-ounce can cream-style corn
¼ cup chopped green pepper
1 tablespoon chopped canned
   pimiento
½ teaspoon salt
   Dash ground cloves
• • •
¼ cup fine dry bread crumbs
2 tablespoons butter *or*
   margarine, melted

In saucepan cook onion wedges, covered, in large amount of boiling salted water for 20 minutes; drain. Combine the corn, green pepper, pimiento, salt, and cloves; stir in the onions. Turn into 1½-quart casserole. Toss bread crumbs with butter. Sprinkle over vegetables. Bake at 350° till heated through, 25 to 30 minutes. Makes 8 servings.

Eggplant Parmigiana

Tomato Sauce
1 medium eggplant (1 pound)
¼ cup all-purpose flour
½ teaspoon salt
1 beaten egg
½ cup cooking oil
⅓ cup grated Parmesan cheese
6 slices mozzarella cheese

Prepare the Tomato Sauce. Meanwhile, peel eggplant and cut into ½-inch slices. Combine flour and salt. Dip eggplant into beaten egg, then in flour mixture. Brown in hot oil in large skillet; drain well on paper toweling.

Place one layer of eggplant in 10x6x2-inch baking dish, cutting to fit. Top with *half* of the Parmesan cheese, *half* of the Tomato Sauce, and *half* of the mozzarella cheese. Cut remaining mozzarella into triangles. Repeat the layers, ending with mozzarella cheese triangles on top. Bake at 400° till heated through, 15 to 20 minutes. Serves 6.

Tomato Sauce: In saucepan cook ⅓ cup chopped onion, ¼ cup finely chopped celery, 1 teaspoon parsley flakes, and ½ clove garlic, minced, in 2 tablespoons cooking oil till tender but not brown. Add one 16-ounce can Italian tomatoes; ⅓ cup tomato paste; 1 bay leaf; ½ teaspoon salt; ½ teaspoon dried oregano, crushed; and ¼ teaspoon pepper. Simmer the tomato mixture gently, uncovered, 45 to 50 minutes. Remove the bay leaf.

Mustard-Glazed Carrots

These tangy carrots are shown on page 78 —

7 or 8 medium carrots
2 tablespoons butter *or* margarine
¼ cup packed brown sugar
2 tablespoons prepared mustard
¼ teaspoon salt
1 tablespoon snipped parsley

Bias-slice carrots about ½ inch thick. Cook carrots, covered, in small amount of boiling salted water till just tender, about 20 minutes; drain. Meanwhile, melt butter in skillet. Stir in brown sugar, mustard, and salt. Add cooked carrots; heat, stirring constantly, till carrots are nicely glazed, about 5 minutes. Sprinkle with parsley. Serves 4.

Scalloped Tomatoes

1 cup chopped celery
½ cup finely chopped onion
2 tablespoons butter *or* margarine
2 tablespoons all-purpose flour
1 tablespoon sugar
½ teaspoon salt
½ teaspoon dried marjoram, crushed
Dash pepper
1 28-ounce can tomatoes, cut up
3 slices bread, toasted and cut in 1-inch squares
1 tablespoon grated Parmesan cheese

In a covered saucepan cook chopped celery and onion in butter or margarine until crisp-tender, about 10 minutes. Combine flour, sugar, salt, marjoram, and pepper; blend into the vegetables. Add the undrained tomatoes; cook and stir till mixture thickens and bubbles.

Stir in *half* of the bread squares. Pour into 1½-quart casserole. Bake at 350° for 30 minutes. Top the casserole with the remaining bread squares and sprinkle with the Parmesan cheese. Bake 20 minutes more. Serve tomatoes in sauce dishes. Makes 6 servings.

Turnip Puff

4 medium turnips
2 tablespoons butter *or* margarine
2 beaten eggs
¾ cup soft bread crumbs (1 slice bread)
1 tablespoon finely chopped onion
1 tablespoon snipped parsley
1 tablespoon sugar
1 teaspoon salt
1 teaspoon lemon juice

Peel and cube turnips (measure about 3 cups). Cook, covered, in small amount of boiling salted water till tender, about 20 minutes. Drain. Add butter and mash. In bowl combine eggs, bread crumbs, onion, parsley, sugar, salt, and lemon juice. Add mashed turnips; mix well. Turn into ungreased 3-cup casserole. Bake at 375° till set, 25 to 30 minutes. Garnish with a sprig of parsley, if desired. Serves 4.

Apple-Zucchini Salad Bowl

    1 tablespoon sesame seed
    ¼ cup mayonnaise *or* salad
        dressing
    ¼ cup French salad dressing
    1 teaspoon sugar
    1 teaspoon vinegar
    ¼ teaspoon salt
        • • •
    6 cups torn lettuce
        (1 small head)
    ¼ cup chopped green pepper
    2 tablespoons sliced green
        onion with tops
    1 cup coarsely chopped
        unpeeled red apple
    ½ cup thinly sliced
        unpeeled zucchini

In small skillet toast sesame seed till lightly browned; set aside. Combine mayonnaise, French dressing, sugar, vinegar, and salt; add sesame seed. In salad bowl combine lettuce, green pepper, and onion; top with the apples and zucchini. Pour the salad dressing atop. Toss salad lightly. Makes 6 servings.

Cucumber-Tomato Salad

    ½ cup cream-style cottage
        cheese with chives
    ¼ cup dairy sour cream
    1 tablespoon lemon juice
    ¼ teaspoon garlic salt
    2 cups thinly sliced unpeeled
        cucumbers
    ¼ cup chopped green pepper
        Lettuce
    2 medium tomatoes, cut in wedges

In large bowl combine the cottage cheese with chives, sour cream, lemon juice, and garlic salt. Add the cucumbers and green pepper; toss to coat. Arrange cucumbers on bed of lettuce; garnish with tomato wedges. Serves 5 or 6.

◀ **Make the most of your food dollar** by selecting fresh vegetables in season. *Cucumber-Tomato Salad*, *Apple-Zucchini Salad Bowl*, and *Mustard-Glazed Carrots* (see recipe, page 77) are all great-tasting recipes within your food budget.

Pickled Onion Rings and Carrots

Delectable meal accompaniment shown on page 66—

    3 medium carrots
    ¾ cup water
    ¾ cup vinegar
    ⅓ cup sugar
    3 inches stick cinnamon,
        broken
    1½ teaspoons mustard seed
    ¼ teaspoon salt
    ¼ teaspoon whole cloves
    1 small sweet onion, thinly
        sliced and separated into
        rings (¼ cup)

Peel carrots and cut in 2½- to 3-inch lengths. In small saucepan simmer carrots in a small amount of boiling water for 5 minutes. Drain the carrots thoroughly; cut into thin sticks.

    In saucepan combine the ¾ cup water, vinegar, sugar, stick cinnamon, mustard seed, salt, and whole cloves. Simmer the mixture, covered, 10 minutes. Strain liquid, discarding spices. Combine carrots and onion rings in a bowl. Pour hot mixture over. Cool to room temperature. Cover and refrigerate the mixture 8 hours or overnight. Drain well. Makes 2 cups.

Sweet-Sour Coleslaw

Colorful cabbage salad shown on page 66—

    5 cups shredded green *or*
        red cabbage
    ⅓ cup finely chopped onion
    ½ cup mayonnaise *or* salad
        dressing
    2 tablespoons sweet pickle relish
    1 tablespoon sugar
    1 tablespoon vinegar
    ½ teaspoon salt
    ½ teaspoon celery seed

In large bowl combine the shredded cabbage and chopped onion. Set aside. Blend together the mayonnaise or salad dressing, pickle relish, sugar, vinegar, salt, and celery seed, stirring till the sugar is completely dissolved. Pour the dressing over the cabbage mixture; toss lightly to coat. Just before serving, sieve hard-cooked egg yolk over top of the salad, if desired. Makes 6 servings.

Honey-Cracked Wheat Bread

Nutty-flavored bread shown on page 69 —

   3½ to 4 cups all-purpose flour
   1 cup cracked wheat
   2 packages active dry yeast
   1¼ cups water
   ½ cup milk
   ⅓ cup honey
   3 tablespoons butter *or* margarine
   1 tablespoon salt
   1 cup whole wheat flour

In mixing bowl combine *2 cups* of the all-purpose flour, cracked wheat, and yeast. Heat together water, milk, honey, butter, and salt just till warm (115-120°), stirring constantly. Add to dry mixture in mixing bowl. Beat at low speed of electric mixer for ½ minute, scraping sides of bowl constantly. Beat 3 minutes at high speed. By hand, stir in whole wheat flour and enough remaining all-purpose flour to make a moderately stiff dough.

Knead on lightly floured surface till smooth and elastic (8 to 10 minutes). Shape into a ball. Place in lightly greased bowl; turn once. Cover; let rise in warm place till double (about 1 hour). Punch dough down; divide in half. Cover; let rest 10 minutes. Shape *each half* into a loaf; place in greased 8½x4½x2½-inch loaf pan. Cover; let rise till almost double (about 45 minutes). Bake at 375° for 35 to 40 minutes. (If crust browns too quickly, cover loosely with foil the last 15 minutes.)

Remove from pans; cool on rack. Brush tops with melted butter, if desired. Makes 2.

Golden Corn Bread

   1 cup all-purpose flour
   1 cup yellow cornmeal
   ¼ cup sugar
   2 teaspoons baking powder
   1 egg
   1 cup milk
   ¼ cup butter *or* margarine, melted

Combine flour, cornmeal, sugar, baking powder, and 1 teaspoon salt. Combine egg, milk, and butter; add to dry ingredients. Stir till moistened. Pour batter into well-greased 8x8x 2-inch baking pan. Bake at 400° till golden brown, 20 to 25 minutes. Makes 8 or 9 servings.

Quick Onion Muffins

   2 cups packaged biscuit mix
   2 tablespoons butter *or*
      margarine, softened
   2 tablespoons chopped green
      onion tops *or* chives
   1 beaten egg

In small bowl combine biscuit mix, butter, and chopped onion tops; mix well. Combine beaten egg and ⅔ cup water; add all at once to biscuit mixture. Stir just till combined. Fill greased or paper bake cup-lined muffin pans ⅔ full. Bake at 400° for 15 to 18 minutes. Serve warm with butter, if desired. Makes 10.

Graham Brown Bread

   1¾ cups all-purpose flour
   2 cups crushed graham crackers
   2 teaspoons baking powder
   1 teaspoon baking soda
   1 teaspoon salt
   ¼ teaspoon ground cloves
   ¼ teaspoon ground nutmeg
   ¼ teaspoon ground cinnamon
   ½ cup shortening
   1¾ cups buttermilk *or* sour milk
   ¾ cup light molasses
   2 beaten eggs
   ¾ cup raisins

In large bowl thoroughly stir together the flour, graham cracker crumbs, baking powder, soda, salt, ground cloves, nutmeg, and cinnamon. Cut in the shortening till mixture resembles coarse crumbs. Combine buttermilk, molasses, and eggs; add to flour mixture, stirring just till moistened. Stir in the raisins. Using greased and floured cans or pan, turn batter into eight 10- to 11-ounce soup cans, *or* six 16-ounce fruit or vegetable cans, *or* one 9x5x3-inch loaf pan. (If you don't have enough cans to bake loaves all at once, cover and refrigerate extra batter. As bread is baked, cooled, and re-moved from cans, wash, grease, and flour cans, then fill again with remaining batter.

Bake at 350° for 35 to 40 minutes for soup or vegetable cans; 60 to 65 minutes for loaf pan. Let cool 5 minutes; remove from pans. Cool completely on wire rack. Makes 6 or 8 small loaves or 1 large loaf.

Banana Bread Pudding

Subtly spiced dessert shown on page 66 —

> 2 bananas, sliced
> 2 tablespoons lemon juice
> 6 slices day-old white bread
> ¼ cup butter, softened
> ½ cup sugar
> 1 teaspoon ground cinnamon
> ½ teaspoon ground nutmeg
> 4 beaten eggs
> 2 cups milk
> 1 teaspoon vanilla

Toss the banana slices with the lemon juice; set aside. Trim crusts from bread, if desired. Spread slices with butter. Cut into ½-inch cubes. Arrange *half* of the bread in 10x6x2-inch baking dish; top with *half* of the banana slices. Repeat with remaining bread and banana slices. Combine sugar, cinnamon, and nutmeg; set aside 2 tablespoons for topping. Combine eggs, milk, vanilla, and remaining sugar-spice mixture. Pour over bread and bananas. Sprinkle reserved 2 tablespoons sugar-spice mixture over top. Set baking dish in shallow baking pan on oven rack; pour hot water around the dish in pan to depth of 1 inch. Bake at 350° till knife inserted in the center comes out clean, 50 to 55 minutes. Serve warm with dollops of red currant jelly, if desired. Serves 8.

Ruby Poached Apples

Baked apple dessert shown on page 66 —

> 2 cups cranberry-apple drink
> 1 3-ounce package cherry-flavored gelatin
> 8 medium baking apples, peeled and cored
> 8 inches stick cinnamon
> 8 whole cloves

In saucepan heat cranberry-apple drink to boiling; add gelatin, stirring to dissolve. Place apples upside down in 12x7½x2-inch baking dish. Pour syrup over apples. Add cinnamon and cloves. Bake, covered, at 325° for 30 minutes. Turn apples upright; spoon syrup over. Cover; bake till done, 20 to 25 minutes more. Remove spices. Serve warm or cool with dollops of cream cheese, if desired. Makes 8 servings.

Caramel-Pecan Dessert Sauce

> 1 cup packed brown sugar
> 2 tablespoons cornstarch
> ¼ teaspoon salt
> ½ cup water
> ¾ cup light cream
> ¼ cup light corn syrup
> ½ cup coarsely chopped pecans
> 2 tablespoons butter *or* margarine
> 1 tablespoon rum *or* brandy

In heavy saucepan combine brown sugar, cornstarch, and salt; stir in water. Stir in light cream and corn syrup. Cook, stirring constantly, till thickened and bubbly. (Mixture may appear curdled during cooking.) Stir in pecans, butter, and rum. Serve warm or chilled on pear halves filled with vanilla ice cream, or serve the sauce over slices of pound cake. Makes 2⅓ cups sauce.

Saucy Banana Dumplings

> Pastry for 2-crust 9-inch pie
> 2 to 3 firm ripe bananas
> 2 tablespoons lemon juice
> ¼ cup sugar
> ¼ teaspoon ground cinnamon
> Milk
> Orange Sauce

Roll the pie pastry to 16x8-inch rectangle. Cut into eight 4-inch squares. Peel and cut bananas in eight 1½-inch pieces; dip in the lemon juice. Combine sugar and cinnamon. Place a banana piece on each pastry square; sprinkle each with *1 teaspoon* of the sugar mixture. Moisten edges of pastry. Bring corners to center; pinch edges to seal. Brush dumplings with a little milk; sprinkle each with ½ *teaspoon* of the remaining sugar mixture. Place dumplings on baking sheet. Bake at 425° for 12 to 15 minutes. Serve immediately with hot Orange Sauce. Makes 4 servings.

Orange Sauce: In saucepan combine ¼ cup sugar and 1 tablespoon cornstarch. Stir in 1 cup orange juice; cook and stir till mixture thickens and bubbles. Remove from heat; stir in 1 tablespoon butter or margarine and 2 teaspoons lemon juice.

Slow Crockery Cooking

Sausage Chili

1 pound bulk pork sausage
1 pound ground beef
1 cup chopped onion
1 cup chopped green pepper
1 cup sliced celery
2 15½-ounce cans red kidney beans
1 28-ounce can tomatoes, cut up
1 6-ounce can tomato paste
2 cloves garlic, minced
2 teaspoons salt
2 teaspoons chili powder

In skillet cook sausage and ground beef till browned; drain off excess fat. Transfer meat to a slow electric crockery cooker. Stir in the remaining ingredients. Cover and cook on low-heat setting for 8 to 10 hours *or* high-heat setting for 4 to 5 hours. Serves 10 to 12.

Mulligatawny

Use Crockery-Stewed Chicken (see recipe, page 84) to prepare the chicken broth and the chicken —

4 cups chicken broth
1 16-ounce can tomatoes, cut up
2 cups chopped cooked chicken
1 tart apple, peeled and chopped
¼ cup finely chopped onion
¼ cup chopped carrot
¼ cup chopped celery
¼ cup chopped green pepper
1 tablespoon snipped parsley
2 teaspoons lemon juice
1 teaspoon sugar
1 teaspoon curry powder
2 whole cloves

In a slow electric crockery cooker combine chicken broth, undrained tomatoes, chicken, apple, onion, carrot, celery, green pepper, and snipped parsley. Combine lemon juice, sugar, curry powder, cloves, ¾ teaspoon salt, and dash pepper; stir into mixture. Cover and cook on low-heat setting for 8 to 10 hours *or* high-heat setting for 4 to 5 hours. Remove cloves before serving. Makes 6 servings.

Borsch-Style Stew

1½ to 2 pounds beef short
    ribs, cut up
1 tablespoon cooking oil
4 carrots, sliced (2 cups)
3 turnips, peeled, sliced, and
    cut in strips (1½ cups)
2 medium beets, peeled, sliced,
    and cut in strips (2 cups)
1 medium onion, sliced (1 cup)
1 cup sliced celery
3 cups water
1 6-ounce can tomato paste
1 tablespoon salt
1 tablespoon sugar
1 tablespoon vinegar
¼ teaspoon pepper
1 small head cabbage, cut
    in 6 wedges
Dairy sour cream

In a large skillet brown the short ribs in hot cooking oil. Drain off the excess fat. Place the sliced carrots, turnips, beets, onion, and celery in the bottom of a low electric crockery cooker. Place short ribs atop the vegetable mixture. Stir together the water, tomato paste, salt, sugar, vinegar, and pepper; mix well. Pour the mixture over the ribs. Cover the crockery cooker and cook on the low-heat setting for 10 to 12 hours *or* on high-heat setting for 5 to 6 hours. Just before serving, skim off the excess fat.

Fifteen minutes before serving, cook cabbage wedges in a 3-quart saucepan in a large amount of boiling salted water till tender, 10 to 12 minutes. Drain the wedges well. Transfer ribs, vegetables, and cabbage to individual soup bowls. Pass sour cream to spoon atop each serving. Makes 6 servings.

Borsch-Style Stew takes care of itself in a ▶ crockery cooker. The long simmering enhances the flavor of the vegetables and the beef becomes fork-tender. Accompany this hearty dish with black bread and beer for a tasty meal.

Spaghetti Sauce Italiano

1 pound ground beef
½ pound bulk Italian sausage
1 28-ounce can tomatoes, cut up
2 6-ounce cans tomato paste
1 6-ounce can sliced mushrooms,
drained
½ cup Burgundy
1 cup chopped onion
¾ cup chopped green pepper
½ cup sliced pimiento-stuffed
green olives
3 bay leaves
2 cloves garlic, minced
1½ teaspoons Worcestershire
sauce
1 teaspoon sugar
1 teaspoon salt
½ teaspoon chili powder
2 tablespoons cold water
2 tablespoons cornstarch
Hot cooked spaghetti
Grated Parmesan cheese

In skillet brown the ground beef and sausage; drain off fat. Transfer meat to a slow electric crockery cooker. Add undrained tomatoes, tomato paste, mushrooms, Burgundy, and ½ cup water. Stir in onion, green pepper, olives, bay leaves, garlic, Worcestershire, sugar, salt, chili powder, and ⅛ teaspoon pepper. Cover and cook on low-heat setting for 10 to 12 hours.

To serve, turn to high-heat setting. Heat till bubbly, 10 minutes; blend cold water slowly into cornstarch; stir into tomato mixture. Cover and cook 10 minutes longer. Serve over spaghetti. Pass Parmesan cheese. Serves 8 to 10.

Corned Beef in Beer

Reserve the flavorful cooking liquid to use as the broth in your favorite vegetable soup recipe—

In a slow electric crockery cooker place 6 potatoes, peeled and quartered; 3 medium onions, peeled and quartered; and 1 cup thinly sliced carrots. Trim off the excess fat from one 3- to 4-pound corned beef brisket; place atop vegetables. Pour 1 cup beer over all. Cover and cook on low-heat setting till tender, 9 to 11 hours. Place meat on warm platter and serve with vegetables. Makes 6 servings.

Crockery-Stewed Chicken

When a recipe calls for cooked chicken and broth, put your electric crockery cooker to work—

In a slow electric crockery cooker combine 4 cups water; 1 bay leaf; 1 teaspoon salt; ¼ teaspoon pepper; ¼ teaspoon dried thyme, crushed; ¼ teaspoon dried marjoram, crushed; and ¼ teaspoon celery salt. Place one 4-pound ready-to-cook stewing chicken, cut up; 4 celery stalks with leaves, cut up; 1 small onion, sliced; and 2 sprigs of parsley. Cover and cook on low-heat setting for 8 to 10 hours *or* on high-heat setting for 4 to 4½ hours.

Remove chicken from crockery cooker, and strain the chicken broth. Set chicken and broth aside to cool. When chicken is cool enough to handle, remove meat from bones. Discard the bones and skin. Cover and store the chicken and broth separately in tightly covered containers in the refrigerator. Makes 4 cups cooked chicken and 4 cups chicken broth.

Scandinavian Pot Roast Dinner

1 11-ounce package mixed dried
fruit
½ cup finely chopped onion
⅓ cup finely chopped carrot
1 clove garlic, minced
1 3-pound beef chuck pot roast
¼ cup Burgundy
¼ cup all-purpose flour

In a slow electric crockery cooker place fruit, onion, carrot, garlic, and ½ cup cold water. Trim excess fat from roast. Cut roast in half and fit into cooker atop fruit mixture. Sprinkle with 1½ teaspoons salt and ¼ teaspoon pepper; pour Burgundy over roast. Cover and cook on low-heat setting for 8 to 10 hours *or* on high-heat setting for 4 to 5 hours.

Remove meat and fruit; pour liquid into bowl; reserve. Return meat and fruit to cooker to keep warm. Skim off excess fat from reserved liquid; add water to make 1½ cups. Pour into saucepan. Blend ½ cup cold water slowly into flour; stir into liquid. Cook gravy, stirring constantly, till thickened and bubbly.

Place meat on platter; top with fruit. Pour some of gravy over; pass the remaining gravy. Makes 6 to 8 servings.

Pizza Swiss Steak

Trim fat from one 2-pound beef round steak cut 1 inch thick. Cut into 6 equal pieces. Combine 2 tablespoons all-purpose flour, 2 teaspoons salt, and ¼ teaspoon pepper. Coat meat with flour mixture; pound to ⅓-inch thickness.

In skillet brown the meat slowly on both sides in 2 tablespoons hot cooking oil; drain off fat. Place 1 medium onion, thinly sliced and separated into rings, in bottom of a slow electric crockery cooker. Place meat atop. Stir together one 8-ounce can tomato sauce, one 8-ounce can pizza sauce, ½ cup water, ½ teaspoon sugar, and ½ teaspoon dried oregano, crushed; pour over meat. Cover and cook on low-heat setting for 8 to 10 hours. Serve over hot cooked spaghetti. Makes 6 servings.

Barbecued Beef Sandwiches

   1 2-pound beef chuck pot roast
   1 15-ounce can tomato sauce
   ¾ cup chopped onion
   ¼ cup chopped green pepper
   2 tablespoons packed brown sugar
   2 tablespoons Worcestershire
      sauce
   1 tablespoon dry mustard
      Dash bottled hot pepper sauce
   1 tablespoon mixed pickling
      spices
   2 tablespoons all-purpose flour
      Individual hard rolls

Trim excess fat from roast. Cut roast in half and fit in bottom of a slow electric crockery cooker. Stir together tomato sauce, onion, green pepper, brown sugar, Worcestershire, dry mustard, hot pepper sauce, and 1 teaspoon salt; pour over meat. Tie pickling spices in cheesecloth bag; add to meat mixture. Cover; cook on low-heat setting for 10 to 12 hours.

Turn cooker to high-heat setting. Lift roast and spice bag from sauce. Skim off excess fat. Remove meat from bone; discard bone and spice bag. Cool meat slightly; cut across grain in thin slices. Heat till bubbly, 10 minutes; blend ¼ cup cold water slowly into flour; stir into sauce. Return meat to cooker. Cover and cook 10 minutes longer. Fill hard rolls with meat mixture. Makes 15 to 20 sandwiches.

Greek-Style Pot Roast

   1 3-pound beef chuck pot roast
   ½ teaspoon grated lemon peel
   ½ cup lemon juice
   3 cloves garlic, minced
   1 teaspoon salt
   1 teaspoon dried oregano, crushed
   ⅛ teaspoon pepper
   ½ cup cold water
   2 tablespoons all-purpose flour
      Hot cooked rice

Trim excess fat from roast. Cut roast in half and fit into the bottom of a slow electric crockery cooker. Stir together lemon peel, lemon juice, garlic, salt, oregano, and pepper. Spoon over the roast.

Cover and cook on low-heat setting for 8 to 10 hours. Remove roast and pour cooking liquid into bowl. Return roast to cooker and cover to keep warm. Skim off excess fat from cooking liquid; add water to make 2 cups. Pour into saucepan. Blend cold water slowly into flour; stir into liquid. Cook gravy, stirring constantly, till thickened and bubbly. Place meat on platter; pour some of the gravy over. Serve remaining gravy over rice. Serves 6 to 8.

Carrot-Pineapple Roast Dinner

In a slow electric crockery cooker place 1 cup thinly sliced carrots. Trim the excess fat from one 3-pound beef chuck pot roast. Cut roast in half and fit into cooker atop carrots. Sprinkle with salt and pepper. Combine one 8¼-ounce can crushed pineapple, undrained; 2 tablespoons packed brown sugar; 2 tablespoons soy sauce; 1 clove garlic, minced; and ½ teaspoon dried basil, crushed. Spoon over roast.

Cover and cook on low-heat setting for 8 to 10 hours. Remove roast. Drain carrots and pineapple; reserve cooking liquid. Return meat, carrots, and pineapple to cooker; cover to keep warm. Skim off fat from reserved liquid; add water to make 1¾ cups. Pour into saucepan. Blend ¼ cup cold water slowly into 2 tablespoons all-purpose flour; stir into liquid. Cook gravy, stirring constantly, till thickened. Place meat on platter; top with carrots and pineapple. Pour some of gravy over; serve remaining gravy over hot cooked noodles. Serves 6.

Hot Potato-Ham Salad

  8 medium potatoes, cooked,
      peeled, and cubed (5 cups), *or*
  3 16-ounce cans sliced
      potatoes, drained
  1 cup chopped fully cooked ham
            • • •
  1 11-ounce can condensed
      cream of celery soup
  ½ cup finely chopped onion
  ¼ cup vinegar
  2 tablespoons sweet pickle relish
  2 tablespoons chopped canned
      pimiento
  1 tablespoon sugar
  ¾ teaspoon celery seed
  ½ teaspoon salt

Place potatoes and chopped ham in a slow electric crockery cooker. In a small bowl combine cream of celery soup, onion, vinegar, pickle relish, pimiento, sugar, celery seed, and salt. Mix together thoroughly. Stir into the potato-ham mixture. Cover and cook on low-heat setting for 4 to 6 hours. Serves 6.

Crock-Style Beans

  1 pound dry navy beans (2½ cups)
  8 cups water
            • • •
  4 ounces salt pork cut in
      small pieces (1 cup)
  1 cup chopped onion
  ½ cup light molasses
  ¼ cup packed brown sugar
  1 teaspoon dry mustard

Rinse beans; place beans in large saucepan and add the water. Bring to boiling; reduce heat and simmer, covered, for 1 hour. Remove from heat and pour into a bowl; cover and refrigerate overnight. Drain beans, reserving the cooking liquid; measure 1 cup for low-heat cooking *or* 1½ cups for high-heat cooking.

  Place beans in the bottom of a slow electric crockery cooker. Stir in reserved cooking liquid, salt pork, onion, molasses, sugar, and mustard. Cover and cook on low-heat setting for 12 to 14 hours *or* on high-heat setting for 5 hours. Before serving, stir through the beans. Makes 6 servings.

Fruit-Filled Squash

  2 small or medium acorn squash
  1 cup chopped apple
  ½ teaspoon grated orange peel
  1 medium orange, peeled and
      diced (½ cup)
  ½ cup packed brown sugar
  4 teaspoons butter *or* margarine

Cut squash in half crosswise; remove seeds. Sprinkle cavities with salt. Combine apple, orange peel, orange, brown sugar, and ½ teaspoon salt. Spoon equal amounts into the four squash cavities; dot each with *1 teaspoon* of the butter. Wrap each securely in foil. Pour ¼ cup water into the bottom of a slow electric crockery cooker. Stack squash, cut side up, in cooker. Cover and cook on low-heat setting for 6 hours. Unwrap; place squash on platter. Drain any syrup remaining in foil into a small pitcher. Serve with squash. Makes 4 servings.

Apricot-Spiced Sweet Potatoes

  6 medium sweet potatoes
  ½ cup packed brown sugar
  ½ cup orange juice
  ¼ cup snipped dried apricots
  ⅛ teaspoon ground cloves
  1 tablespoon butter *or* margarine

In saucepan cover and cook potatoes in large amount of boiling salted water till tender, 40 minutes. Cool; peel and quarter. Combine brown sugar, orange juice, apricots, cloves, and ¼ cup water. Pour into the bottom of a slow electric crockery cooker; stir in potatoes.

  Cover and cook on high-heat setting for 3 hours. Turn into a mixing bowl; beat butter into mixture till nearly smooth. Serves 8.

Cranberry-Spiced Toddy

In a slow electric crockery cooker combine one 32-ounce bottle cranberry juice cocktail, 2 cups orange juice, 1 cup unsweetened grapefruit juice, 1 cup apple juice *or* cider, ½ cup grenadine syrup, ¼ teaspoon ground cloves, and ¼ teaspoon ground nutmeg. Cover and heat the mixture on low-heat setting for 4 to 6 hours. Serve hot in mugs. Makes 8 (8-ounce) servings.

Hot Buttered Lemonade

In a slow electric crockery cooker combine 9 cups hot water, 1¾ cups sugar, 1 tablespoon shredded lemon peel, and 1½ cups lemon juice. Cover and heat on low-heat setting for 4 to 6 hours. Pour into mugs; top each with 1 teaspoon of butter. Makes 12 (8-ounce) servings.

Regal Plum Pudding

     3 slices bread, torn in pieces
     1 5⅓-ounce can evaporated milk
     2 ounces beef suet, ground
     ¾ cup packed brown sugar
     1 beaten egg
     ¼ cup orange juice
     ½ teaspoon vanilla
     1½ cups raisins
     ¾ cup snipped pitted dates
     ½ cup diced mixed candied
          fruits and peels
     ⅓ cup chopped walnuts
     ¾ cup all-purpose flour
     1½ teaspoons ground cinnamon
     ¾ teaspoon baking soda
     ¾ teaspoon ground cloves
     ¾ teaspoon ground mace
          Fluffy Hard Sauce

Soak bread in evaporated milk and beat to break up. Stir in suet, brown sugar, egg, orange juice, and vanilla. Combine raisins, dates, candied fruits and peels, and nuts. Stir together the flour, cinnamon, soda, cloves, mace, and ¼ teaspoon salt; add to fruit mixture and mix well. Stir in bread-suet mixture. Turn into a well-greased 3-pound shortening can. Cover the top of the can with foil and tie foil on tightly with string.

Place can on a rack (use a metal jar lid or crumpled foil) in the bottom of a slow electric crockery cooker. Cover and cook on high-heat setting for 3½ hours. Remove the can from cooker; cool 10 minutes before removing the pudding from can. Serve warm with Fluffy Hard Sauce. Makes 12 servings.

Fluffy Hard Sauce: In a small mixing bowl thoroughly cream together 2 cups sifted powdered sugar and ½ cup butter *or* margarine. Beat in 1 egg yolk and 1 teaspoon vanilla. Fold in 1 stiffly beaten egg white into mixture. Chill.

Cinnamon-Spiced Applesauce

     4 pounds tart cooking apples,
          peeled, cored, and thinly
          sliced (12 cups)
     ½ cup sugar
     ½ teaspoon ground cinnamon
     1 cup water
     1 tablespoon lemon juice

In a slow electric crockery cooker place the sliced apples. Combine the sugar and ground cinnamon; mix thoroughly with apples. Add water and lemon juice. Cover and cook on low-heat setting for 5 to 7 hours *or* on high-heat setting for 2½ to 3½ hours. Makes about 6 cups.

Golden Fruit Compote

     1 29-ounce can peach *or*
          pear slices
     ¾ cup orange juice
     ½ cup dried apricots
     ¼ cup light raisins
     ⅛ teaspoon ground cinnamon
     ⅛ teaspoon ground nutmeg

In a slow electric crockery cooker combine undrained peaches, orange juice, apricots, raisins, cinnamon, and nutmeg. Stir mixture, making sure syrup covers the fruit. Cover; cook on low-heat setting for 6 to 8 hours. Serves 6.

Pink Squirrel Fondue

     2 7-, 9-, or 10-ounce jars
          marshmallow créme
     ⅓ cup creme d'almond
     2 tablespoons white créme de
          cacao
     1 tablespoon lemon juice
          Strawberry, banana, and
          pound cake dippers

In a slow electric crockery cooker combine the marshmallow creme, crème d'almond, white crème de cacao, and lemon juice. Cover and cook on high-heat setting for 30 minutes; stir occasionally. Serve at once or reduce heat and keep warm, covered, on low-heat setting for 1 to 2 hours; stir occasionally.

Spear dipper with fondue fork; dip into the fondue, swirling to coat. Serves 10 to 12.

Make Leftovers Work for You

Broccoli and Ham Sauce

Spoon over Cheese Biscuits, as shown on page 66 —

  1 10-ounce package frozen
      cut broccoli
  ¼ cup butter *or* margarine
  ¼ cup all-purpose flour
  2 cups milk
  1 tablespoon Worcestershire
      sauce
  2 teaspoons instant minced
      onion
  ¼ teaspoon salt
      Dash cayenne pepper
  1½ cups cubed fully
      cooked ham
      Cheese Biscuits

Cook broccoli according to package directions; drain. In saucepan melt butter; blend in flour. Stir in milk, Worcestershire sauce, onion, salt, and cayenne. Cook and stir till thickened and bubbly. Stir in ham and drained broccoli. Heat through. Serve over hot, split Cheese Biscuits. Makes 4 servings.

Cheese Biscuits

  2 cups all-purpose flour
  1 tablespoon baking powder
  ½ teaspoon salt
  ¼ cup shortening
  1 egg
  ¾ cup milk
  ½ cup shredded American cheese

In mixing bowl stir together flour, baking powder, and salt. Cut in shortening till mixture resembles coarse crumbs. Make a well in center. Beat together egg and milk; add all at once to flour mixture. Stir in cheese. Stir with fork just till dough clings together. Knead gently on lightly floured surface (10 to 12 strokes). Roll or pat to ½-inch thickness. Cut with 2½-inch biscuit cutter. Place on ungreased baking sheet. Bake at 450° till golden, 10 to 12 minutes. Split and serve hot with Broccoli and Ham Sauce. Makes 10.

Stuffed Zucchini

  2 medium zucchini (1 pound)
  ¼ cup finely chopped onion
  1 tablespoon butter *or* margarine
  ½ cup cream-style cottage cheese
  ½ cup cooked rice
  ½ cup chopped fully cooked ham
  1 beaten egg
  1 tablespoon snipped parsley
  ⅛ teaspoon dried basil, crushed
  2 slices sharp American cheese,
      cut in 16 strips (2 ounces)

Wash zucchini; trim ends. Cook in boiling water just till tender, 8 to 10 minutes. Halve lengthwise. Remove centers; dice to make ¾ cup. Set shells aside. Cook onion in butter till tender. Stir in diced zucchini, cottage cheese, rice, ham, egg, parsley, basil, ¼ teaspoon salt, and dash pepper. Lightly salt zucchini shells; fill with ham mixture. Place in 12x7½x2-inch baking dish. Bake, covered, at 350° for 25 minutes. Place *4 cheese strips* on each. Bake, uncovered, 2 to 3 minutes. Serves 4.

Saturday Meat Loaf

  2 beaten eggs
  ¾ cup milk
  ⅔ cup fine dry bread crumbs
  2 tablespoons finely chopped
      onion
  1 teaspoon salt
  ¼ teaspoon chili powder
      Dash pepper
  1½ pounds ground beef
  ¼ cup hot-style catsup
  1 tablespoon brown sugar
  ½ teaspoon dry mustard

Combine eggs, milk, crumbs, onion, salt, chili powder, and pepper. Add beef; mix well. Pat mixture into 8x1½-inch round baking dish. Bake at 350° for 1 hour. Drain excess fat. Combine catsup, brown sugar, and dry mustard; spread over meat loaf. Return to oven for 10 minutes. Cut into wedges. Makes 6 servings.

Stretching one meal into two is the result of good planning. For example, this hearty *Corn Bread-Pork Bake* combines yesterday's chopped pork with crumbled corn muffins. Crisp bacon and sage help add new flavor. Round out the meal with a tossed salad.

Corn Bread-Pork Bake

    3 slices bacon
    ½ cup finely chopped celery
    2 tablespoons chopped onion
    1 cup pork gravy *or* 1 envelope
        chicken gravy mix
    1 cup finely chopped cooked pork
    2 cups coarsely crumbled
        corn bread or muffins
    1 cup dry bread cubes
    ¼ teaspoon rubbed sage

In skillet cook bacon till crisp; drain, reserving drippings, and crumble. To drippings in skillet, add celery, onion, and ¼ cup water. Cover; cook till vegetables are tender, about 7 minutes. Stir gravy into vegetables, *or* add 1 cup water to gravy mix; stir in. Bring to a boil. Simmer 1 minute; stir constantly. Combine bacon, pork, corn bread, bread cubes, sage, and gravy mixture. Turn into a 1-quart casserole. Cover; bake at 350° for 35 minutes. Top with additional bacon, if desired. Serves 4.

Oniony Ham and Cheese Chowder

    2 medium potatoes, peeled and
        cubed (2 cups)
    1 cup chopped onion
    3 tablespoons butter *or* margarine
    3 tablespoons all-purpose flour
        Dash pepper
    3 cups milk
    1½ cups chopped fully cooked ham
    1½ cups shredded sharp American
        cheese (6 ounces)
        Toasted croutons (optional)

Cook potatoes in ½ cup boiling water till tender, about 10 minutes. Drain, reserving liquid. Add enough water to make 1 cup. In saucepan cook onion in butter till tender but not brown. Blend in flour and pepper. Add milk and potato water all at once. Cook and stir till mixture thickens and bubbles. Add chopped ham and shredded cheese; stir to melt cheese. Ladle into soup bowls. Serve with toasted croutons, if desired. Makes 8 servings.

Turkey-Broccoli Bake

A company-special casserole using cooked turkey—

  2 10-ounce packages frozen
    chopped broccoli
  1 tablespoon lemon juice
  2 tablespoons butter *or* margarine
  2 tablespoons all-purpose flour
  ½ teaspoon salt
  2 cups milk
  ½ cup shredded Swiss cheese
  2 cups cooked turkey cut in
    strips
  ½ cup soft bread crumbs
  ¼ cup grated Parmesan cheese
  1 tablespoon butter *or* margarine,
    melted

Cook broccoli according to package directions. Drain well; mix with lemon juice. Place in an 8x1½-inch round baking dish. In saucepan melt 2 tablespoons butter. Blend in flour and salt. Add milk all at once. Cook, stirring constantly, till mixture thickens and bubbles. Remove from heat; stir in the Swiss cheese till melted. Stir in turkey. Spoon over broccoli. Sprinkle with mixture of bread crumbs, Parmesan cheese, and 1 tablespoon butter. Bake at 350° till heated through, 20 to 25 minutes. Serves 6.

Turkey Round-Up

Hearty grilled sandwiches for lunch—

  ½ cup mayonnaise *or*
    salad dressing
  1 tablespoon chopped dill pickle
  1 teaspoon finely chopped onion
 12 slices bread
  6 slices Swiss cheese
  6 slices salami
  6 slices tomato
  6 slices cooked turkey
  6 tablespoons butter *or*
    margarine, softened

Combine mayonnaise, dill pickle, and onion. Spread on one side of each bread slice. Top 6 bread slices with one slice *each* of Swiss cheese, salami, tomato, and turkey. Cover with remaining bread slices, mayonnaise side down. Spread butter on outside of sandwiches. Grill on low heat of griddle, turning once, till brown, 10 to 12 minutes. Makes 6 sandwiches.

Hollandaise Turkey Slices

  8 slices cooked turkey
  1 teaspoon instant chicken
    bouillon granules
  3 tablespoons butter *or* margarine
  ¼ cup all-purpose flour
  ¾ cup milk
  1 3-ounce can sliced mushrooms
  2 egg yolks
  1 tablespoon lemon juice
  ¼ cup butter *or* margarine, melted

Place turkey in a 10x6x2-inch baking dish. Dissolve bouillon in 1 cup boiling water; set aside. In saucepan melt the 3 tablespoons butter; blend in flour and ¼ teaspoon salt. Add bouillon and milk all at once. Cook and stir till thickened and bubbly. Drain mushrooms and stir into sauce. Pour over turkey. Bake at 350° till heated through, about 15 minutes. Meanwhile, beat egg yolks till thick and lemon-colored. Add lemon juice, ¼ teaspoon salt, and dash pepper. Gradually beat in the ¼ cup melted butter. Pour over turkey. Broil till golden, 1 to 2 minutes. Makes 8 servings.

Curried Turkey Open-Facers

  1 large red apple, cored
    Lemon juice
 12 thin slices cooked turkey
  2 tablespoons turkey broth *or*
    water
  ½ of a 10½-ounce can condensed
    cream of chicken soup (⅔ cup)
  ¼ cup dairy sour cream
  3 tablespoons milk
  2 teaspoons curry powder
  6 slices French bread, toasted

Cut apple into thin wedges; brush with lemon juice. In skillet heat turkey in broth, covered, for 4 to 5 minutes; turn slices once. Meanwhile, in saucepan combine soup, sour cream, milk, and curry powder; heat through. Place 2 slices turkey and 3 apple wedges atop each slice of bread; spoon sauce over. Serves 6.

Thin Apple wedges are the surprise ingredient ▶ in *Curried Turkey Open-Facers.* The curry sauce topping has a soup and sour cream base.

One-Crust Frozen Pot Pies

½ cup finely chopped celery
½ cup finely chopped onion
¼ cup snipped parsley
3 tablespoons butter *or* margarine
3 tablespoons all-purpose flour
¼ teaspoon salt
⅛ teaspoon pepper
3 cups chicken, turkey, *or*
   beef broth
2 cups diced, cooked beef, pork,
   chicken, or turkey, *or* 1 9-ounce
   can tuna, drained and flaked
½ cup cooked peas
½ cup diced cooked carrots
   Pastry for 1-crust 9-inch pie

In saucepan cook celery, onion, and parsley in butter till tender. Blend in flour, salt, and pepper. Stir in broth. Cook and stir over medium heat till mixture is thickened and bubbly. Combine sauce with cooked meat, peas, and carrots; cover and chill thoroughly. Divide cooled mixture evenly among six 4½x1-inch pie pans. Prepare pastry; divide into 6 equal portions. Roll each to a 5-inch circle. Place one atop each pie; seal to edge of pan. Wrap pies separately in heavy foil; seal, label, and freeze.

To serve, unwrap and cut slits in top crust. Place on baking sheet. Do not thaw; bake frozen pie at 425° till golden, about 40 minutes. Cover edges with foil the last 10 minutes if necessary to prevent overbrowning. (Bake unfrozen pies 20 to 25 minutes.) Serves 6.

Potato-Spinach Combo

1 10-ounce package frozen
   chopped spinach
   Packaged instant mashed
   potatoes (enough for 4
   servings) *or* 2 cups cooked
   potatoes
½ cup dairy sour cream

In medium saucepan cook frozen spinach according to package directions. Remove from pan; drain well. In same pan prepare potatoes according to package directions, *except* decrease water by 3 tablespoons. Stir in sour cream, spinach, and dash pepper. Heat through over low heat. Makes 6 servings.

Pineapple Bread Pudding

¼ cup butter *or* margarine
4 slices day-old bread
1 8½-ounce can pineapple tidbits
1 13-ounce can evaporated milk
2 beaten egg yolks
½ cup sugar
½ teaspoon ground nutmeg
1 teaspoon vanilla
2 egg whites
¼ teaspoon cream of tartar

Soften butter; spread on both sides of bread slices. Cut into ½-inch cubes; set aside. Drain pineapple; reserve syrup. Combine syrup and milk. (Add water, if needed, to make 2 cups.) Blend with egg yolks, ¼ *cup* of the sugar, nutmeg, and ½ *teaspoon* of the vanilla. Fold in pineapple and bread cubes. Divide among six 6-ounce custard cups. Place cups in baking pan on oven rack. Pour boiling water in pan around cups to depth of 1 inch. Bake at 350° till knife inserted off-center comes out clean, about 20 minutes.

Meanwhile, beat egg whites, cream of tartar, and remaining ½ teaspoon vanilla to soft peaks. Slowly add remaining ¼ cup sugar, beating to stiff peaks. Spread over hot pudding; seal to edge of cups. Bake till meringue browns, 12 to 15 minutes. Serve warm or cool. Serves 6.

Cinnamon-Rice Doughnuts

1 beaten egg
1 cup cooked rice
½ cup milk
1 tablespoon cooking oil
1 cup all-purpose flour
2 tablespoons granulated sugar
1½ teaspoons baking powder
1 teaspoon ground cinnamon
⅛ teaspoon salt
   Fat for frying
   Powdered sugar

Blend egg, rice, milk, and oil. Combine flour, granulated sugar, baking powder, cinnamon, and salt. Stir into egg mixture just till moistened. Drop batter by rounded teaspoonfuls into deep hot fat (375°). Fry till golden, about 1½ minutes per side. Drain on paper toweling. Dip in powdered sugar. Serve hot. Makes 24.

INDEX
A-B

D-F

G-O